CAVENDISH PRACTI

Child Care and Protection

SECOND EDITION

BARBARA MITCHELS

LLB, DIP COUNSELLING & PSYCHOTHERAPY,
CHILDREN PANEL SOLICITOR

SERIES EDITOR
CM BRAND, SOLICITOR

Cavendish
Publishing
Limited

First published by Longman Law, Tax and Finance.

Second edition published in Great Britain 1996 by Cavendish Publishing Limited, The Glass House, Wharton Street, London WC1X 9PX

Telephone: 0171-278 8000 Facsimile: 0171-278 8080

© Cavendish Publishing Ltd 1996

All rights reserved. No part of this publication may be reproduced, stored in a retrieval system, or transmitted in any form or by any means, electronic, mechanical, photocopying, recording or otherwise, without the prior permission of the publisher.

Any person who infringes the above in relation to this publication may be liable to criminal prosecution and civil claims for damages.

No responsibility for loss occasioned to any person acting or refraining from action as a result of the material in this publication can be accepted by the author, editors or publishers.

Mitchels, Barbara
Child Care and Protection Law and Practice – 2nd edn – (Practice Notes series)
1. Children – Legal status, Laws, etc – England
I. Title
344.2'04327

ISBN 1 85941 292 0

Printed and bound in Great Britain

Preface

Child care and protection is a vast area of law, and practitioners do not usually have the time to read all the academic material on offer. This book endeavours to provide a basic practical guide through the maze of the Children Act 1989 and its subordinate legislation, guidance and case law.

Child care and protection practice is not just a matter of law. We also need to understand the work of social services and other agencies involved in child protection, and how to generate action on behalf of our child clients. We often need to know where to find information and how to locate experts who can help in case preparation. The first time in court as advocate or witness can be daunting, and it helps to know a little about court procedure in advance.

Children are wonderful clients. It is a privilege to work with them, and with their families.

Barbara Mitchels
July 1996

Acknowledgments

Many thanks to all those who have given permission to include quotations, references, and material; and to the children and families who are better sources of information than any law book!

Especial thanks to John, Ruth, Jo, and Anne Marie, for their tolerance, encouragement, patience, and endless cups of tea whilst this was being written!

Contents

1 Sources and Introduction to the Children Act 1989
1.1 Statutes 1
1.2 Statutory instruments 2
1.3 Case law 3
1.4 Practice directions 3
1.5 Guidance 3
1.6 Official publications 4
1.7 Basic definitions 4
1.8 Orders available under the Children Act 1989 12
1.9 Introduction to the Children Act 1989 13

2 Taking Instructions in Family Law Cases
2.1 Action plan on receipt of instructions 15
2.2 Interviewing clients 16

3 Principles underlying the Children Act 1989
3.1 Paramountcy of the welfare of the child 24
3.2 Delay is deemed prejudicial to child's interests 25
3.3 No order unless necessary in the interests of the child 26

4 Parental Responsibility
4.1 Definition, powers and duties of parental responsibility 27
4.2 Legal position of child's natural mother 30
4.3 Legal position of child's father 31
4.4 Acquisition and loss of parental responsibility by the child's natural father 31
4.5 Acquisition of parental responsibility by others 35

5 Child Protection Procedures in Health and Social Work
5.1 Hierarchy within social services departments 37
5.2 Referral procedures and preliminary investigations 38

5.3	Child protection conferences	40
5.4	Child protection register	42
5.5	Assessment of risk	44
5.6	Child protection plan	44
5.7	Local authority duty to promote welfare of children in their area	45

6 Emergency Protection Orders
6.1	Effects of order	48
6.2.	Duration	49
6.3.	Grounds for application	49
6.4	Practice and procedure	50
6.5	Contact, accommodation, and the rights of the child	51
6.6	Variation and discharge	52

7 Child Assessment Orders
7.1	Effects of order	54
7.2.	Grounds for application	54
7.3	Practice and procedure	55
7.4	Contact, accommodation, and the rights of the child	56
7.5.	Appeals, variation and discharge	57

8 Care and Supervision Proceedings
8.1.	Effects	59
8.2	Grounds for application for a care or supervision order	59
8.3	Practice and procedure	60
8.4	Significant harm	64
8.5	Interim orders	64
8.6	Effects of care order	66
8.7	Effects of supervision order	69
8.8	Removal of child from care	72
8.9	Variation, discharge and appeals	73

9 Secure Accommodation
9.1	Effects of order	75
9.2	Duration	78
9.3	Grounds for application	79
9.4	Practice and procedure	81
9.5	Role of the guardian *ad litem*	83

9.6	Contact issues	83
9.7	Rights of the child	84
9.8.	Appeals	84

10 Education Supervision Orders
10.1	Effects	86
10.2	Duration	87
10.3	Grounds for application	87
10.4	Practice and procedure	88
10.5	Rights of the child	89
10.6.	Variation, discharge and appeals	90

11 Police Powers under the Children Act 1989   91

12 Case Preparation and Advocacy in Child Law
12.1	Preparation of the case	92
12.2.	Burden of proof in child law cases	92
12.3	Special evidence rules in child law cases	92
12.4	Directions hearings – ordering the evidence	94
12.5	Court procedure at the hearing	94
12.6.	Courtroom skills	98

13 Children's Rights
13.1	To accept or refuse medical treatment	101
13.2	To accept or refuse medical or psychiatric assessment	103
13.3	To make his or own application to the court	104
13.4	To disagree with the guardian a*d litem* and instruct a solicitor separately	104
13.5	Rights of a child in care	105

14 Other Children Act Orders available to the Court
14.1	Orders in family proceedings	106
14.2	Section 8 orders	106
14.3	Contact	110
14.4	Prohibited steps	111
14.5	Residence	111
14.6	Specific issue	112
14.7	Supplementary provisions	112

14.8	Practice and procedure in s 8 applications	113
14.9	Family assistance order	116
14.10	Order to local authority to investigate under s 37 Children Act	117

15 Commencement and Transfer of Proceedings
15.1	General rules	118
15.2	Specified exceptions to the general rules	119
15.3	Transfers	119
15.4	Urgent applications	122

16 Working with Children
16.1	Role of the guardian *ad litem*	123
16.2.	Should I see my child client?	125
16.3	Taking instructions and communicating with children	128
16.4	Child development	130
16.5	Understanding your child client - race, religion, culture and ethnicity	130
16.6	After the case is over	130

17 Legal Aid, Appeals and Enforcement
17.1	Legal aid	132
17.2	Appeals and judicial review	133
17.3	Complaints procedures	136
17.4	Enforcement	136

18 Expert Evidence
18.1	Instructing experts	137
18.2	Finances	139
18.3	Finding the right expert	139

19 Information, Guidance and Reference Works
19.1	Essential information library	141
19.2	Reading and reference list	142

20 Improving Law, Skills and Practice
20.1	Inter-disciplinary associations	145
20.2	The Law Society's Children Panel	146
20.3	Accreditation and family lawyers	146

1 Sources and Introduction to the Children Act 1989

1.1 Statutes

- Abortion Act 1967
- Access to Health Records Act 1990
- Access to Personal Files Act 1987
- Adoption Act 1976
- Child Abduction and Custody Act 1985
- Child Support Act 1991
- Children Act 1989
- Children and Young Persons Act 1933
- Children and Young Persons Act 1969
- County Courts Act 1984
- Courts and Legal Services Act 1990
- Education Act 1944
- Family Law Act 1986
- Family Law Reform Act 1969
- Family Law Reform Act 1987
- Foster Children Act 1980
- Human Fertilisation and Embryology Act 1990
- Local Government (Miscellaneous Provisions) Act 1976
- Mental Health Act 1983
- National Assistance Act 1948
- Police and Criminal Evidence Act 1984
- Rehabilitation of Offenders Act 1974
- Sexual Offences Act 1956

- Supreme Court Act 1981
- Surrogacy Arrangements Act 1985

1.2 Statutory instruments

- Access to Personal Files (Social Services) Regulations 1989, SI 1989/206
- Access to Personal Files (Social Services) (Amendment) Regulations 1991, SI 1991/1587
- Adoption Rules 1984, SI 1984/265
- Arrangements for Placement of Children (General) Regulations 1991, SI 1991/890
- Children (Allocation of Proceedings) Order 1991, SI 1991/1677
- Children (Allocation of Proceedings, Appeals) Order 1991, SI 1991/1801
- Children (Secure Accommodation) Regulations 1991, SI 1991/1505
- Children (Secure Accommodation No 2) Regulations 1991, SI 1991/2034
- Children (Admissibility of Hearsay Evidence) Order 1993, SI 1993/621
- County Court Rules 1981, SI 1981/1687
- Family Proceedings (Amendment) Rules 1991, SI 1991 2113
- Family Proceedings (Amendment) Rules 1992, SI 1992/456
- Family Proceedings (Amendment No 2) Rules 1992, SI 1992/2067
- Family Proceedings (Amendment) Rules 1993, SI 1993/295
- Family Proceedings (Amendment No 2) Rules 1994, SI 1994/2165
- Family Proceedings Courts (Children Act 1989) Rules 1991, SI 1991/1395
- Family Proceedings Rules 1991, SI 1991/1247
- Parental Responsibility Agreement Regulations 1991, SI 1991/1478
- Parental Responsibility Agreement Regulations 1994, SI 1994 /3157
- Children (Secure Accommodation) (No 2) Regulations 1991, SI 1991/2034
- Representations Procedure (Children) Regulations 1991 S1 1991/894
- Review of Childrens' Cases Regulations 1991, SI 1991/895
- Rules of the Supreme Court 1965, SI 1965/1776

1.3 Case law

Case law has been referred to in the text and references cited there. It remains essential to monitor case law developments in this field as new issues are examined in the courts and tested through the appeal process.

1.4 Practice directions

- Family Proceedings (Allocation to Judiciary) Directions 1993 [1993] 2 FLR 1008
- Practice Direction [1993] 1 WLR 313 and 1 All ER 820
- Practice Direction [1993] 1 All ER 820; [1993] 1 FLR 668.
- Practice Direction (Children Act 1989 – Applications by Children) [1993] 1 WLR 313; [1993] 1 All ER 820; [1993] 1 FLR 1008

1.5 Guidance

Current child protection procedures are set out in 'Working Together under the Children Act 1989' (HMSO, 1991) and the Children Act Guidance and Regulations. These are issued under s 7 Local Authority Social Services Act 1970 and therefore, should be followed by local authorities. A local authority must justify any departure from their provisions. Unjustifiable failure to comply may form the basis for complaint or judicial review.

- The Children Act 1989: Guidance and Regulations (available from HMSO)

    | Volume 1 | Court orders   ISBN   0-11-321371-9 |
    | Volume 2 | Family support, day care, and educational provision for young children ISBN 0-11-321372-7 |
    | Volume 3 | Family placements ISBN 0-11-321375-1 |
    | Volume 4 | Residential care ISBN 0-11-321430-8 |
    | Volume 5 | Independent schools   ISBN 0-11-321373-5 |
    | Volume 6 | Children with disabilities ISBN 0-11-321452-9 |
    | Volume 7 | Guardians *ad litem* and other court related issues ISBN 0-11-321471-5 |
    | Volume 8 | Private fostering and miscellaneous ISBN 0-11-321473-1 |

Volume 9   Adoption issues ISBN 0-11-321474-X
Volume 10   Index ISBN 0-11-321538-X
- 'The Care of Children, Principles and Practice in Regulations and Guidance' (HMSO, 1991)
- Introduction to the Children Act 1989 (HMSO, 1991)
- 'Working Together under the Children Act 1989' (HMSO, 1991)

1.6   Official publications

- Report of the Inquiry into Child Abuse in Cleveland 1987
- Home Office Circular 88/1982
- Home Office Circular 105/1982
- Home Office Circular 102/1988
- Home Office Circular 45/91
- Local Authority Circular LAC (88) 23
- Protecting Children – A Guide for Social Workers Undertaking a Comprehensive Assessment', Department of Health (HMSO, 1990)
- 'The Right to Complain' by the Department of Health and Social Services Inspectorate (HMSO, 1991)
- 'Guide to Listing Officers' (Lord Chancellor's Department, September 1991)
- 'Guidance on Acting for Children in Private Law Proceedings under the Children Act 1989' (The Law Society Family Law Committee, 1994)
- Guidance for Solicitors Attending Child Protection Conferences' (The Law Society Family Law Committee, 1995)
- 'Good practice in Family Law on Disclosure' (Solicitors Family Law Association, 1996)
- 'Guide to Good Practice for Solicitors Acting for Children' (Solicitors Family Law Association, 1995)

1.7   Basic definitions

The interpretation of many terms used within the Children Act 1989 are given in s 105. The source of definitions created by other sections, other Acts or by case law are cited.

adoption agency   'a body which may be referred to as an adoption agency by virtue of s 1 of the Adoption Act 1976'.

authorised person	in relation to care and supervision proceedings, means the NSPCC or its officers, under s 31(9)(a), or a person (other than a local authority) authorised by order of the Secretary of State to bring proceedings under s 31 of the Act for a care or supervision order. In practice no-one has been so authorised s 31(9)(b).
authority	the local authority of a geographical area, including County Councils, District Councils, Unitary authorities in England and Wales, Welsh County Councils, Welsh County Borough Councils.
care order	an order made under s 31(1)(a), placing a child in the care of a local authority. By s 31(11), this includes an interim care order made under s 38. And by s 105 any reference to a child who is in the care of an authority is a reference to a child who is in their care by virtue of a care order.
child	a person under the age of 18.
child assessment order	an order under s 43 of the Act to produce the child and to comply with the court's directions relating to the assessment of the child. There are restrictions on keeping the child away from home under this section.
child in care	a child in the care of a local authority pursuant to an order made under s 31(1)(a) or an interim order under s 38 of the Children Act.
child in need	By s 17 Children Act , 'a child is taken to be in need if: (a) he is unlikely to achieve or maintain, or to have the opportunity of achieving or maintaining, a reasonable standard of health or development without the provision for him of services by a local authority; (b) his health or development is likely to be significantly impaired or further impaired, without the provision for him of such services; or (c) he is disabled'.
child minder	is defined in s 71 Children Act as a person who looks after one or more children under the age

of eight, for reward; for total period(s) exceeding two hours in any one day. A person is not deemed to provide day care for children unless the total period(s) during which the children are looked after exceeds two hours in any day.

child of the family
'in relation to the parties to a marriage, means (a) a child of both of those parties (b) any other child, not being a child who is placed with those parties by a local authority or voluntary organisation, who has been treated by both of those parties as a child of their family'.

child looked after by a local authority
is a child who is in the care of a local authority by virtue of a care order, or provided with accommodation by a local authority.

child provided with accommodation by a local authority
is a child who is provided with accommodation by a local authority in the exercise of its functions which stand referred to their social services committee under the Local Authorities Social Services Act 1970 (includes children in what was previously called 'voluntary care').

children's home
defined in s 63 as a home which usually provides or is intended to provide care and accommodation wholly or mainly for more than three children at any one time. Obviously many homes contain three or more children, and the section lists several exceptions, including the homes of parents, relatives, or those with parental responsibility for the children in question.

community home
is defined in s 53, and may be '(a) a home provided, equipped and maintained by a local authority, or (b) provided by a voluntary organisation but in respect of which ... the management, equipment and maintenance of the home shall be the responsibility of the local authority; ... or the responsibility of the voluntary organisation'.

contact order
defined in s 8(1) as 'an order requiring the person with whom a child lives, or is to live, to

	allow the child to visit or stay with the person named in the order, or for that person and the child otherwise to have contact with each other'.
development	defined in s 31(9) as physical, intellectual, emotional, social or behavioural development.
disabled	defined in s 17(11) and 'in relation to a child, means a child who is blind, deaf, or dumb or who suffers from mental disorder of any kind or who is substantially and permanently handicapped by illness, injury or congenital deformity or such other disability as may be prescribed.'
education supervision order	means an order under s 36(1) of the Act, putting the child with respect to whom the order is made under the supervision of a designated local education authority.
emergency protection order	Under s 44 of the Act, this order:

'(a) operates as a direction to any person ... in a position to do so to comply with any request to produce the child ...

(b) authorises:

   (i) the removal of a child to accommodation provided by or on behalf of the applicant, and his being kept there; or

   (ii) the prevention of the child's removal from any hospital or other place in which he was being accommodated immediately before the making of the order; and

(c) gives the applicant parental responsibility for the child.'

family assistance order	an order made under s 16 of the Act appointing a probation officer or an officer of the local authority to advise assist and (where appropriate) befriend any person named in the order for a period of six months or less. Named persons may include parents, guardians, those with whom the child lives, or the child himself.
family proceedings	is defined in s 8(3) as any proceedings:

(a) under the inherent jurisdiction of the High Court in relation to children; and

(b) under Parts I, II and IV of the Act; the Matrimonial Causes Act 1973; the Domestic Violence and Matrimonial Proceedings Act 1976; the Adoption Act 1976; the Domestic Proceedings and Magistrates' Courts Act 1978; ss 1 and 9 of the Matrimonial Homes Act 1983; and Part III of the Matrimonial and Family Proceedings Act 1984, also under s 30 HFEA 1990.

guardian — means a guardian appointed under s 5 of the Act for the child, but not for the child's estate.

guardian *ad litem* — officer of the court with a duty to report to the court on the best course to be taken in the interests of the child. See ss 41–42, and the Children Act Guidance vol 7.

harm — is defined in s 31(9) and means the ill-treatment or the impairment of health or development. Where the question of whether the harm is significant or not turns on the child's health and development, his health or development shall be compared with that which could be reasonably expected of a similar child, s 31(10).

health — means physical or mental health.

hospital — any health service hospital, and accommodation provided by the local authority and used as a hospital. It does not include special hospitals, which are those for people detained under the Mental Health Act 1983, providing secure hospital accommodation.

ill-treatment — is defined in s 31(9) and includes sexual abuse and forms of ill-treatment which are not physical.

local authority — means a council of a county, a metropolitan district, a London borough, or the Common Council of the City of London; in Scotland, it means a local authority under Social Work (Scotland) Act 1968, s 12.

local authority foster parent — means any person with whom a child has been placed by a local authority under s 23 (2)(a) of the Act. Local authority foster parents may

	include a family; a relative of the child; or any other suitable person.
local housing authority	is as defined in the Housing Act 1944; meaning the District council; London Borough council; Common council of the City of London; or council of the Isles of Scilly.
parent	the natural mother or father of a child, whether or not they are married to each other at the time of the birth or of conception. The Children Act when it says 'parent' means natural parents of a child, including therefore natural fathers without parental responsibility. Where it intends to mean 'a parent with parental responsibility' it says so specifically.
parent (in relation to adoption)	'applicants shall be proposed adopter ... and respondents shall be each parent or guardian ... of the child'. Adoption Rules 1984 (SI 1984/265), r 15: 'parent' has the same meaning as in the Children Act 1989, r 2 amended by the Adoption (Amendment) Rules 1991 (SI 1991/1880). Schedule 10, para 30(7) Children Act provides an amendment to s 72(1) (interpretation) of the Adoption Act 1976 (to which the Adoption Rules are subordinate), that 'parent shall mean 'any person who has parental responsibility for the child under the Children Act 1989' and 'parental responsibility' and 'parental responsibility agreement' shall have the same meanings as under the Children Act 1989. See *Re C (Minors) (Adoption: Residence Order)* [1994] Fam 1 and *M v C and Calderdale Metropolitan Borough Council* [1993] 1 FLR 505 in which the Court of Appeal held that former parents would need leave to apply for s 8 orders after adoption since they are no longer 'parents' under the Children Act.
parent with parental responsibility	All mothers have parental responsibility for children born to them. Married fathers also have parental responsibility. The father of a child who

	is not married to the mother is able to acquire parental responsibility in various ways under the Children Act. This term therefore excludes the natural father of a child who has not yet acquired parental responsibility under the Act
parental responsibility	defined in s 3, and includes all the rights, duties, powers responsibilities, and authority which by law a parent of a child has in relation to the child and his property. It can be acquired by unmarried fathers in respect of their child by order or agreement under the Children Act; and by others through a residence or guardianship order. Parental responsibility can be shared with others. It ceases when the child reaches 18, on adoption or death.
parental responsibility agreement	defined in s 4(1) as an agreement between the father and mother of a child providing for the father to have parental responsibility for the child (a father married to the mother of their child at the time of the birth will automatically have parental responsibility for that child, but a father not so married will not). Format for agreement set out in Parental Responsibility Agreement Regulations 1991, SI 1991/1478, as amended by SI 1994/3157.
private fostering	see s 66 Children Act, to 'foster a child privately' means looking after a child under the age of 16 (or if disabled, 18), caring and providing accommodation for him or her; by someone who is not the child's parent, relative, or who has parental responsibility for the child.
prohibited steps order	defined in s 8(1). Means an order that no step which could be taken by a parent in meeting his parental responsibility for a child, and which is of a kind specified in the order, shall be taken by any person without the consent of the court.
protected child	is a child protected under the Adoption Act 1976, ie a child who is living with the applicant to adopt that child, who has given notice to the local authority of his or her intention to apply to adopt. The child is subject to the super-

	vision of the local authority during the period of protection, which continues until one of a number of specified circumstances occur.
registered children's home	defined in s 63 as a home, registered under the Act, which provides (or usually provides or is intended to provide) care and accommodation wholly or mainly for more than three children, who are not siblings with respect to each other, at any one time. Section 63 provides a number of exceptions to the category of children's homes.
relative	in relation to a child means a grandparent, brother, sister, uncle or aunt (whether of the full blood or of the half blood or by affinity) or step-parent.
residence order	an order under s 8(1) settling the arrangements to be made as to the person with whom a child is to live.
responsible person	defined in Sch 3 para 1. In relation to a supervised child, it means: (a) any person who has parental responsibility for the child; and (b) any other person with whom the child is living.
service	in relation to any provision made under Part III of the Act (local authority support for children and families) means any facility.
special educational needs	These arise when there is a learning difficulty which calls for special educational provision to be made. The Education Act 1981, s 1(1), sets out the meaning of 'learning difficulty'.
specific issue order	means an order under s 8(1) giving directions for the purpose of determining a specific issue which has arisen, or which may arise, in connection with any aspect of parental responsibility for a child.
supervision order	means an order under s 31(1)(b) and (except where express provision to the contrary is made), includes an interim supervision order made under s 38.

supervised child/
supervisor   in relation to a supervision order or an education supervision order, mean respectively the child who is (or is to be) under supervision and the person under whose supervision he is (or is to be) by virtue of the order.

upbringing   in relation to any child includes the care of the child but not his maintenance.

voluntary home   means any home or other institution providing care and accommodation for children which is carried on by a voluntary organisation, with certain exceptions set out in s 60 of the Act.

voluntary organisation means a body (other than a public or local authority) whose activities are not carried on for profit.

1.8 Orders available under the Children Act 1989

Order	Section	Duration*
Parental responsibility	4	Age 18
Guardianship	5	Age 18
Residence	8	Age 16 (18 in exceptional circumstances)
Contact	8	Age 16 (18 in exceptional circumstances)
Prohibited steps	8	Age 16 (18 in exceptional circumstances)
Specific issue	8	Age 16 (18 in exceptional circumstances)
Family assistance	16	Six months
Care order	31	Age 18
Interim care order	38	First, not more than eight weeks; remainder, max four weeks
Supervision	31	Age 18; one year, may be extended to max total three years
Care contact order	34	Duration of care order

Education supervision	36	One year; repeatedly extensible for three years. Ceases at age 16
Child assessment	43	Seven days
Emergency protection	44	Eight days; extensible for further seven days

* These orders may be brought to an end by court order, variaton or discharge, and subject to additional provisions. For details please refer to the relevant chapter.

1.9 Introduction to the Children Act 1989

The Children Act 1989 (referred to below as the Children Act) came into force on 19 October 1991, containing 108 sections and 15 schedules, and accompanied by the Family Proceedings Courts (Children Act 1989) Rules 1991, SI 1991/1395, and Family Proceedings (Children) Rules 1991, SI 1991/910.

The Children Act created a new unified court system consisting of three tiers: the High Court, the county court and the family proceedings court, each of which have concurrent jurisdiction and powers. Appeals from the family proceedings court go to the High Court, and from the county court and High Court to the Court of Appeal and the House of Lords. Cases may move up or down the tiers, transfers therefore being easier. The avoidance of delay is one of the underlying principles of the Children Act. To implement this the Act with its subsidiary rules created a new system of directions hearings to enable the courts to take firmer control of the timing of cases, admission of evidence and administrative matters.

The Children Act encourages families to stay together, imposing a duty on local authorities to provide services for children in need and their families, to reduce the necessity for children to be looked after away from home, and for child protection proceedings. Unless the criteria for the making of care or supervision orders are met, an order cannot be made. The courts have no power to order a child into the care of a local authority of their own volition. The Children Act introduced a new concept of parental responsibility, which unmarried fathers may gain in relation to their children, and accessible to others, eg grandparents or step-parents in conjunction with residence orders. The Children Act creates orders governing aspects of a child's life-contact with others; residence; and resolution of disputed aspects of child care – prohibited steps (forbidding actions) and specific issues (permitting actions to take place).

The powers of the police to remove a child, or to retain a child away from home, are now limited to 72 hours.

The principles behind the Children Act and its guidance are that children are people, whose rights are to be respected, not just 'objects of concern', and that children should wherever possible remain with their families, helped if necessary by provision of services, provided their welfare is safeguarded. An atmosphere of negotiation and co-operation between professionals is encouraged. The welfare of the child is paramount, and in the field of child care and protection, professionals are expected to work together in a non-adversarial way for the benefit of the child.

2 Taking Instructions in Family Law Cases

Family proceedings are non adversarial. Chapter 16 'Working with Children' discusses taking instructions from child clients at para 16.3. Advocates may be instructed by local authorities, parents, or others in family proceedings, and competent advocacy involves thorough preparation of the case, see para 12.1. An advocate needs to elicit from their client as much information as possible about their client's circumstances and those of the child. All evidence relevant to the welfare of the child should be available to the court.

2.1 Action plan on receipt of instructions

- Arrange to interview the client as soon as possible.
- Check the legal aid situation and complete necesssary forms (see para 17.1)
- Ask for copies of applications and documents filed with the court.
- Are there proceedings current or pending? Obtain details.
- Have there been previous proceedings? If so, ask for court orders and copies of documents filed with the court.
- Check who are the parties in the case.
- Ascertain whether other parties have instructed advocates, and obtain details.
- Let the court and other parties, or their advocates if they are represented, know you are instructed in the matter, and write, inviting communication and offering co-operation.
- If there is a guardian *ad litem*, let them know you are instructed (see Chapter 16 if instructed by the guardian *ad litem* on behalf of the child).
- Interview client.
- Interview potential witnesses.
- For subsequent stages in the preparation of a case, see Chapter 12.

2.2 Interviewing clients

Cases involving family breakup or issues of child protection are stressful for all the parties concerned. It is essential to establish a relationship of trust with clients, giving them space in the initial interview to express their feelings, whilst at the same time keeping the interview focussed on taking background history and instructions. Set aside sufficient time to allow clients to fully express all they have to say, and offer appropriate refreshments- a cup of tea can provide a welcome break. A checklist may assist to keep the interview focussed on the information required. Below are reproduced checklists for interviewing parents, social workers, and medical witnesses.

Figure 1: Checklist for information from parents

Full name

Address

Home telephone number (ok to use this?)
Work telephone number (ok to use this?)
Family members living in household with child

Close family members outside household

The family's social/cultural/racial context

Does this client, the family, or the child, have any special needs, cultural issues, language problems, etc?

Education/background/attainments of parents, carers/child(ren)

Does any family member, carer, co-habitee, have any convictions for relevant offences?
eg conviction of offence listed in Sched 1 Children and Young Persons Act 1933 (known colloquially as 'Sched 1offence'); drink or drugs related offences etc?
Convictions should be disclosed to the court: *Re R (Minors) (Custody)* [1986] 1 FLR 6

Does the client or any family member have any particular skills or attributes relevant to their parenting ability?

Have there been any court orders or applications made to a court in respect of a child of the family or any family member?

Other people involved with the family who may be able to assist in providing information:
- schools attended by the child(ren)
- playgroups
- voluntary organisations/religious organisations
- therapists
- GP/hospital
- health visitor

How does the client see the situation; what were the circumstances that led up to this application?

Does the client have explanations to offer about causation of injuries, or the child's emotional problems?

What contact has the client had to date with social services, or other professionals about this child?

What would the client like to see happen?

What would the child(ren) like to happen?

What does the client think that others will say about the situation? (often a very revealing question)

Can the client think of others who may be able to offer information about the child or family?

Figure 2: Checklist for information from social workers

Names and addresses of other potential witnesses

Full name
Office address

Office tel no
Post held

Relevant qualifications

Relevant experience

Reason for involvement with the family, or initial referral to social services department
(check confidentiality, eg does the location of the child require protection, or is there sensitive information in this report?)

Date of initial involvement with child/family

Dates of subsequent involvement, in chronological order, including:
* whom seen
* venues
* duration
* documents referred to
* other contacts, eg by telephone

Description of the composition of immediate and wider family

Put the family in its social/cultural/racial context
Define any special needs, cultural requirements, language problems, etc

Education/background/attainments of parents/carers/siblings where relevant

Does any family member, carer, co-habitee, have any convictions? Details should be obtained and made available for the court

Does any family member have any particular relevant skills/attributes?

Are there any previous court orders or applications made to a court in respect of a child of the family or family member?

Brief chronological outline of formal social work involvement with the family
(case conferences, entries on the Child Protection Register, reviews planning meetings etc)

Other professionals involved with the family:
- schools attended by the child(ren)
- playgroups
- voluntary and/or religious organisations
- therapists
- family aide

Medical history of the child:
- GP
- Health visitor
- Hospital admissions recorded

Observations ... personality, physical appearance and demeanour of the child and characteristics of carers/parents/wider family members where relevant

Home circumstances ...
Observations about the family home, adequacy for family needs (are s 17 or other resources needed here?), attention to needs of child (toys, safety, stimulation etc); food and drink (eg availability and suitability); any relevant factors noted? (eg indications of drug use, alcoholism, etc?)

Outline the presenting problems within this family

Attitudes of the parents/carers/child to presenting problems:
- explanations offered as to causation of injuries
- explanations offered as to causation of emotional problems

With reference to the guidance in the Memorandum of Good Practice in child interviews:
- how does the child perceive these events?
- who did the child tell about these events?
- how did the child tell about them?
  (does (s)he tell you, draw pictures, etc)

(social workers should note carefully any responses made – at or as soon as possible after their visits to the family, make these notes and present them in chronological order and have the originals available at court)

In your view, can the parents/carers control the child ?
(if not, how does the lack of control show, and what are the apparent reasons?)

History of the action(s) taken by social services and others to assist and protect this child and family so far, given in chronological order

Attitude of family/child to the provision of services/protection measures

Bearing in mind the Children Act criteria in s 31, is there an assessment of:
- the past harm to the child
- current harm to the child
- future risk of harm to the child?

Options for consideration, see the list of court orders in the Sources list at 1.3.

What are the wishes and feelings of the family in relation to the options discussed with them?

What are the wishes and feelings of the child(ren) about the options discussed with them?

Which is the preferred option for social services point of view acting in the best interests of the child?

Care plan (bearing in mind the Guidance Family Placements Vol 3 at pp 15–16 para 2.62)

Written agreements (bearing in mind the Guidance Family Placements Vol 3 at pp 16–17 para 2.63)

Any action(s) need to be carried out before the plan can be put into action? (eg are assessments needed? Do parents/carers /child need to comply with requests to do something?) Anything likely to adversely affect implementation of the care plan?

Other relevant considerations

Bear in mind the welfare checklist

Ensure that any opinions expressed are objective, relevant, and supported by observations

Figure 3: Checklist for information from medical witnesses

Witness' full name
Health Centre/Surgery/Hospital address
Post held
Relevant qualifications and experience
Nature, extent, venue and duration of examination(s) of the child/family: • date, duration and venue of first examination   • reason for referral   • observations of child on examination ...   • appearance, demeanour, attitude to examination and others present   • note any statements made by the child or by others that are relevant   • any abnormalities in physical or mental state   • marks, abrasions, wounds, skeletal survey, pain, tenderness,   • unusual features or appearance of any part of the body
Body map showing location of areas of injury, bruising, etc can be very helpful
Colour photographs are of great help to a court if the child/family is willing to allow this, but beware, if sexual abuse is alleged, photography may remind child of the abuse or be further abusive
Description of the general health of the child
Full description of the child's injuries/abnormalities, with an explanation of the medical terms used
Is it possible to give a time of the occurrence of the injuries?
When the injuries occurred, would they have caused pain to the child? Would (s)he have cried out, screamed in pain? Does it still hurt? How soon afterwards would it stop hurting? Should a caring adult have noticed/treated the child's discomfort/pain?

Were there attempts to treat the injuries/or to cover them up?
Is there any evidence of brittle bones or other congenital factor likely to contribute to these injuries or explain them?

If anyone was asked about the injuries, note who was asked, who was present, their reactions to the question, the questions used, and the responses given. Demeanour is often relevant here. Did anyone give an explanation of how the injuries/abnormalities occurred?

Does any explanation given by adults agree/conflict with the diagnosis?

What is the prognosis?

Date(s), venue and duration of subsequent examinations

Significant health issues within family including parents, brothers, sisters, other children

Health history of the child ... in chronological order including:
- physical development

- height/weight/centile charts

- developmental assessments according to age

- visual /hearing/ neurological/speech /language assessments

- evidence of emotional problems/abnormalities (have they been diagnosed as a congenital or naturally occurring disorder, or is there possibly some other cause? If so, any clues as to what?)

- evidence of physical problems/abnormalities (do they constitute an illness or disability? Have they been diagnosed as a congenital or naturally occurring disorder, or is there possibly some other cause? If so, any clues as to causation ?)

- treatment(s) given to the child

- what was the effect of treatment?

- advice offered to the family/child about medical care
- was the advice taken up and acted upon?

Up-to-date information about the child where is (s)he at physically/ developmentally, now?

Other information that is relevant for the case conference or the court to know

The witness should bear in mind the welfare checklist when writing their statement, it is a useful guide to how the court or a case conference will be thinking and approaching the best interests of the child

Names and addresses of doctors, other professionals who have been involved with the child/family who may be able to give relevant information. Any other Doctors/Consultants to whom child referred for specialist treatment or examination

'Dates to avoid' ... times when not available to come to court, conferences, meetings

3 Principles underlying the Children Act 1989

3.1 Paramountcy of the welfare of the child

The Children Act 1989 (referred to below as the 'Children Act') commences with a clear direction in s 1(1) that:

> When a court determines any question with respect to:
> (a) the upbringing of a child; or
> (b) the administration of a child's property or the application of any income arising from it,
> the child's welfare shall be the paramount consideration.

The court must have regard to the criteria set out in s 1(3) Children Act, known as the 'welfare checklist', when considering an application to vary or discharge an order under Part IV (a child protection order) or a contested s 8 order for contact, residence, specific issue or prohibited steps.

The welfare checklist is not compulsory in other circumstances, but it is always useful for practitioners to consider it. If expert reports refer to these criteria, they are complying with the principles of the Act.

3.1.1 The welfare checklist

- The ascertainable wishes and feelings of the child concerned (considered in the light of his age and understanding).
- Her physical, emotional and educational needs.
- The likely effect on him of any change in his circumstances.
- Her age, sex, background and any characteristics of hers which the court considers relevant.
- Any harm which he is suffering or which he is at risk of suffering.

- How capable each of her parents, and any other person in relation to whom the court considers the question to be relevant, is of meeting her needs.
- The range of powers available to the court under this Act in the proceedings in question.

A number of cases discuss the welfare checklist. It has been held irrelevant in applications for leave to seek a s 8 order, where the criteria in s 10(9) apply. These are not substantive hearings under the Act, see *North Yorkshire CC v G* [1993] 2 FLR 732. However, if the child is the applicant for leave, then s 10(9) does not apply and the welfare principle is operative, *Re C (Minor)* [1994] 1 FLR 96.

The guardian *ad litem* most often advises the court on the child's welfare in cases under Part IV of the Act, see para 16.1, below.

In private law cases (those between individuals as opposed to those involving State intervention in a family's life), the court may ask the court welfare officer to investigate the child's circumstances and to report back to the court the child's wishes and feelings, also advising the court on the best way to safeguard the child's welfare.

The court should be alert to any unusual circumstances or factors of concern in private law cases, even if the parties themselves are in agreement. The court may order a welfare officer's report, or direct the local authority to investigate a child's circumstances under s 37 Children Act, or make s 8 or s 16 (family assistance) orders of its own volition if necessary.

In *Birmingham CC v H* [1994] 1 All ER 12; 1 FLR 224 the court held that in a Part IV application concerning a child whose parent was herself still a minor, the welfare of the child subject to the application was paramount.

3.2. Delay is deemed prejudicial to child's interests

> In any proceedings in which any question with respect to the upbringing of a child arises, the court shall have regard to the general principle that any delay in determining the question is likely to prejudice the welfare of the child (s 1(2) Children Act).

The court regulates the timing of cases by *directions* or *preliminary hearings*. In these, the court establishes who are parties to, or who should have notice of, the proceedings. The court ensures that the evidence is in order and service is carried out. A timetable is set for preparation and disclosure of evidence to other parties and the guardian *ad litem*, and a hearing date fixed. Directions given carry the force of court orders, failure to comply with them will be viewed by the court seriously, and a full explanation for non-compliance will be required. Sanctions include wasted costs orders against those parties to a case who cause (or negligently allow) unnecessary delay. See *Ridelhalgh v Horsfield* and *Watson v Watson* [1994] 3 WLR 462; [1994] 3 All ER 848; [1994] 2 FLR 194 for the Court of Appeal's guidance on wasted costs.

3.3 No order unless necessary in the interests of the child

The Act assumes that the parties will do their best to resolve differences by negotiation and co-operation. Section 1(5) Children Act provides that the court has a positive duty not to make an order unless it is in the interests of the child to do so. This is referred to as the 'non-intervention' principle. See *Re W* [1994] 2 FCR 1216, in which the Court of Appeal discussed this principle in an application for a contact order.

4 Parental Responsibility

On 19 October 1991 the Children Act 1989 (referred to below as the 'Children Act') changed the status of parents in relation to their children. Parents (or anyone else), in order to make decisions for a child, now need to have parental responsibility for that child.

Parental responsibility may be shared with others. It is exerciseable by each person who has it individually, without a duty to consult the others, with certain exceptions.

4.1 Definition, powers and duties of parental responsibility

Section 3(1) Children Act defines parental responsibility as:

> All the rights, duties, powers, responsibilities and authority which by law a parent of a child has in relation to the child and his property.

This wonderfully vague definition is not clarified anywhere in the Children Act except in s 3(2) which states that parental responsibility includes the powers of a guardian in looking after a child's property, eg to give a valid receipt for a legacy. Paragraph 1.4 of *Introduction to the Children Act 1989* HMSO says: 'That choice of words emphasises that the duty to care for the child and to raise him to moral, physical, and emotional health is the fundamental task of parenthood and the only justification for the authority it confers.'

Volume 1 *Guidance and Regulations* (Court Orders) para 2.2 says that parental responsibility is concerned with bringing the child up, caring for him, and making decisions about him, but does not affect the relationship of parent and child for other purposes. It does not affect rights of maintenance or succession.

Some statutory powers are reliant upon parental responsibility:
- Appointment of guardian for a child in the event of death; s 5(3) Children Act.

- Consent to the adoption of the child; s 16 Adoption Act 1976.
- Access to the child's medical records; ss 4, 5, and 12 Access to Health Records Act 1990.
- Consent to a child's marriage; s 1 Marriage Act 1941 as amended by Sched 12 para 5 Children Act.
- Consent of all those with parental responsibility or leave of the court is required for removal of a child from the country, failing which a criminal offence is committed; s 1 Child Abduction and Custody Act 1985.

This provision applies even if there is a residence order in force, but under s 13(2) Children Act, the person holding a residence order in his or her favour may take the child abroad for holiday purposes for up to one month. The court may, of course, grant additional or general leave to take the child abroad for longer periods or permanently.

Powers and duties of those with parental responsibility include:

- Lawful correction. It is a defence to assault or to a charge of ill treating a child under s 1 Children and Young Persons Act 1933 for a parent to prove that the act was one of 'lawful correction'.
- Application for or veto of child's passport; *Practice Direction* [1986] 1 All ER 977 at p 9821 and *Re A* [1995] 1 FLR 767.
- Right to represent child as 'next friend' in all court proceedings where the child is a party except cases involving child protection or the upbringing of the child. The right can be removed if the parents act improperly or against the interests of the child, RSC Ord 80 r 2, CCR Ord 10 r 1.
- Right to name or re-name child. If both parents have parental responsibility, and they agree, there is no problem. If only one has parental responsibility then it is submitted that she would have the sole right to make the name change. Disagreement between those with parental responsibility should be resolved by s 8 order – specific issue or prohibited steps. Section 13(1) Children Act forbids name changes if a residence order is in force without consent of all those with parental responsibility for the child or leave of the court.
- Parents' right to decide child's education, and duty to send their child to school, or to provide suitable alternative schooling, Education Acts 1962 and 1944. Schedule 13 para 10 Children Act includes those who are not parents but who have parental responsibility for the child. See *Re Z (Minor) (Freedom of Publication)* [1996] 2 WLR 107; 1 FLR 191, on education, medical consent and publication of information.

- Decisions about a child's religion. The courts will not interfere unless the welfare of the child is threatened.
- Consent to medical assessment, examination or treatment.
- 'Nearest relative' in the Mental Health Act 1983 s 27(2) is now amended to substitute for the word 'mother' both the mother and the father who has parental responsibility within the meaning of s 3 Children Act.

4.1.1 Duration

Parental responsibility lasts until a child is 18 years old if it belongs to the mother or the married father of the child, or to the father of the child by virtue of a parental responsibility agreement, legitimation, or a court order. Parental responsibility can be acquired along with residence orders or guardianship. See below at 4.4.3. and 4.4.4.

4.1.2 Parental responsibility and medical consent

Medical records should record who has parental responsibility for children. With unmarried parents, in the absence of a parental responsibility agreement or court order, only the mother will have parental responsibility for the child. Should she (or any lone person with parental responsibility) die, there will be no one with parental responsibility for the child. Single parents should therefore appoint a guardian for their child.

No person may be given medical treatment without consent. Whatever the motivation, this may constitute an assault for which practitioners may incur liability in tort or criminal law. Detention in hospital or any other place without consent could constitute false imprisonment.

In emergencies, where there is no person capable or available to give or withhold consent, the doctor may lawfully treat the patient.

Young people of 16 plus
Section 8 Family Law Reform Act 1969 confers on a person of 16 the right to give informed consent to surgical, medical, or dental treatment. Examinations or assessments could also impliedly be included. Those who suffer mental illness, disability, or psychiatric disturbance will be subject to the same mental health provisions and safeguards as adults.

Children under 16
In *Gillick v West Norfolk and Wisbech Area Health Authority* [1986] AC 112 Mrs Gillick challenged her local health authority's provision of

contraceptive advice to her daughters under 16 without her consent. The House of Lords supported the health authority's actions. In giving judgment, it formulated the concept known colloquially as '*Gillick* competence'. A child under 16 may make medical decisions according to her chronological age, in conjunction with mental and emotional maturity, intelligence, comprehension and the quality of the information provided to her.

In the case of *Re R (Minor: Consent to Medical Treatment)* [1992] Fam 11; [1992] 1 FLR 190 CA, the Court of Appeal held that a '*Gillick* competent' child acquires a right to make decisions equal to that of each of his parents, and only the absence of consent by all having that power would create a veto. If they cannot agree, then the doctor lawfully may act on consent of one. However, *A Guide to Consent for Examination or Treatment*, National Health Service Management Executive, advises that the refusal of an adult or competent young person must be respected.

If there is disagreement or refusal concerning medical treatment for a child when a doctor considers it necessary, and negotiation fails, then the matter can be resolved by specific issue order, see para 15.6. The High Court in its inherent jurisdiction or under the Children Act can override the wishes of anyone in relation to a child in the child's best interests.

4.1.3 What if there is no one with parental responsibility?

Where immediate action is needed for the welfare of the child and no one with parental responsibility is available, s 3(5) Children Act provides:

> A person who:
>
> (a) does not have parental responsibility for a particular child; but
>
> (b) has care of the child, may ... do what is reasonable in all the circumstances of the case for the purpose of safeguarding or promoting the child's welfare.

This could apply to child minders, foster carers, neighbours and others looking after children.

4.2 Legal position of child's natural mother

Parental responsibility always belongs to a mother in relation to the children to whom she has given birth. It does not matter whether she is married to the father of the child (or to anyone else) or not. Nothing can remove that parental responsibility from her save for death or adoption of the child.

4.3 Legal position of child's father

4.3.1 Married fathers

Under s 2(1) Children Act a father automatically has parental responsibility for his children if he was 'married to their mother at the time of their birth'. This concept includes marriage at the time of the child's conception *Re Overbury dec'd* [1954] 3 All ER 308. The man must be the biological father. Section 1(2) Family Law Reform Act 1987 includes in the meaning of s 2(1) children legitimated by statute. This enables a child's father to gain parental responsibility if he subsequently marries the child's mother.

A married man has no parental responsibility for children who are not biologically his own, even if they are born during the marriage. Children born to a married couple as a result of artificial insemination will, however, be regarded as the child of the husband provided that the conditions set out in the Human Fertilisation and Embryology Act 1990 are met.

Note that men who become step-parents on marriage do not automatically acquire parental responsibility for their spouses' children.

4.3.2 Unmarried fathers

A father who is not married to the mother of his child has no parental responsibility, but he can acquire it in a number of ways which are set out below.

4.4 Acquisition and loss of parental responsibility by the child's natural father

4.4.1 Parental responsibility order

A father may apply under s 4(1)(a) Children Act for a parental responsibility order.

Applicant The father (no one else can apply).

Parties/respondents All those with parental responsibility (or if a care order is in force, those who had parental

	responsibility immediately prior to that order). On discharge application, all parties to the original proceedings. FPC (CA 1989) 1991 Sched 2 col (iii) and FPR 1991 App 3 col (ii).
Notice	Local authority providing accommodation for the child. Person(s) with whom the child is living at time of application, FPC (CA 1989) 1991 Sched 2 col (iv) and FPR 1991 App 3 col (iv). Person providing certified refuge for the child (see s 51 Children Act).
Status of child	With leave, a child of sufficient age and understanding can oppose the application or apply to set aside the order.
Procedural notes	Family proceedings under Children Act. Application on form C1 or C2 FPC (CA 1989) 1991 Sched 1 and FPR 1991 App 1. Service at least 14 days before date of directions/hearing. Respondents – copy application, date and time of directions/hearing. Notice – notification of application also date and time of hearing. The remaining procedure is the same as for s 8 applications, see Chapter 15.
Attendance	All parties shall attend, unless otherwise directed. The rules make an exception that proceedings shall take place in the absence of any party (including the child) if he is represented by guardian ad litem or solicitor, and it is in the child's interests having regard to the issues or evidence. FPC (CA 1989) 1991 r 16(2). and FPR 1991 r 4.16(2).
Issues for the court	Degree of attachment between father and child. Commitment shown by father to child. The reasons for the application (not improper or wrong). Children Act principles – welfare of child paramount; no delay; no order unless it is in best interests of child to make it.

Relevant cases: *Re G (Minor) (Parental responsibility)* [1994] 1 FLR 504; *Re T (Minor) (Parental Responsibility)* [1993] 2 FLR 450.

4.4.2 Parental responsibility agreement with the mother

The mother and father may agree that the father shall have parental responsibility for the child. The agreement must be made in accordance with the Children (Parental Responsibility Agreement) Regulations 1991 as amended, SI 1991/1478 and SI 1994/3157.

The prescribed form is straightforward, and must be completed, signed by the mother and father, and witnessed by a court officer or justices' clerk. Some courts ask the parents to produce the child's birth certificate, and evidence of their own identity incorporating their signature and photograph. (See figure 4, p 34.)

4.4.3 Residence order

A child's father may acquire a residence order under s 8 Children Act. This may be granted on application or of the court's own volition in the course of family proceedings, see Chapter 15.

The court has power to award parental responsibility with residence orders which subsists while the order remains in force. Residence orders expire by effluxion of time when the child reaches 16, unless there are exceptional circumstances, in which case it can be extended to age 18.

However, there are special provisions in the Children Act when the father of a child acquires a residence order relating to his child. On making the residence order, the court must also grant parental responsibility to the father, under s 4 and s 12(1) Children Act . The court shall not bring that parental responsibility order to an end whilst the residence order remains in force. The parental responsibility so granted will not expire with the residence order (eg when the child reaches 16) but will last until the child is 18, unless the court specifically brings the father's parental responsibility to an end earlier, s 91(7) Children Act .

4.4.4 Guardianship

The court may appoint a guardian for a child under s 5 Children Act where:

- there is no person with parental responsibility for the child; or
- a residence order has been made in favour of a parent or guardian who died whilst the order was in force.

This parental responsibility subsists until the child reaches 18, unless ended earlier by the court, s 91(7).

Figure 4: Form from the Children (Parental Responsibility Agreement) Regulations 1991 as amended, SI 1991/1478 and SI 1994 /3157

	This is a Parental Responsibility Agreement regarding	
the Child	Name	
	Boy or Girl Date of birth Date of 18th birthday	
Between the Mother	Name Address	
and the Father	Name Address	
	We declare that we are the mother and father of the above child and we agree that the child's father shall have parental responsibility for the child (in addition to the mother having parental responsibility).	
	Signed (Mother)	Signed (Father)
	Date	Date
Certificate of Witness	The following evidence of identity was produced by the person signing above:	The following evidence of identity was produced by the person signing above:
	Signed in the presence of Name of Witness	Signed in the presence of Name of Witness
	Address	Address
	Signature of Witness	Signature of Witness
	[A Justice of the Peace] [Justices' Clerk] [An Officer of the Court authorised by the Judge to administer oaths]	[A Justice of the Peace] [Justices' Clerk] [An Officer of the Court authorised by the Judge to administer oaths]

A parent with parental responsibility, or a guardian, may appoint a guardian for a child in the event of his death under s 5(3) and (4) Children Act respectively. If when he dies there is no one else alive with parental responsibility, the appointed guardian will act. If there is anyone with parental responsibility still alive, then the guardian will only be able to act after the death of all others with parental responsibility. If, however, someone with a residence order in her favour appoints a guardian, she will act on the death of the appointer, in conjunction with anyone else remaining alive who has parental responsibility.

4.5 Acquisition of parental responsibility by others

4.5.1 Relatives

Relatives can obtain parental responsibility for a child along with a residence order under s 8 and s 12(2) Children Act.

Relatives could also seek an appointment under s 5 as guardian of the child, which automatically gives them parental responsibility until the child reaches 18 or the court orders otherwise, s 91(7).

A relative could also, in theory, apply to adopt a child in order to gain parental responsibility. Courts will not favour adoption since the effect of adoption is to sever legal ties with anyone else with parental responsibility. It is acceptable sometimes, eg adoption by a grandmother of a young child who was so criminally abused by parents that neither could safely undertake the care of the child.

4.5.2 Step-parents

Step-parents do not acquire parental responsibility for the children of their partners on marriage. Currently, they can only acquire parental responsibility along with a residence order under s 8 and s 12(2) Children Act, or by adoption.

The courts would not normally favour adoption unless the natural father is dead, whether he has parental responsibility or not, since adoption would sever his legal responsibility for, and relationship with, his child.

The mother of a child (who always has parental responsibility herself) may develop terminal illness or die whilst in a relationship with a man who is not the father of her child. The child may be very attached to him, and he may be committed to the care of the child.

If the mother dies, there are three possible scenarios, all potentially difficult:
(a) *The child's genetic father is alive but has no parental responsibility*

   The child will then legally have no one with parental responsibility.

   Remedies:
   - before the mother's death, the stepfather obtains a residence order alone or shared with the mother;
   - mother appoints the stepfather guardian under s 5;
   - if the mother has died, the stepfather obtains a residence order or guardianship order under s 5(1)(a). Guardianship automatically gives him parental responsibility until the child reaches 18 or the court orders otherwise, s 91(7).

(b) *If the child's genetic father is alive and has parental responsibility*

   The the genetic father will then automatically hold the legal responsibility for the child.

   The stepfather can seek a residence order. If he has been appointed as guardian by the mother before her death, this will only be effective immediately if she had a residence order in her favour before her death, s 5 (7)(b) Children Act (see above at 4.4.3). He could seek guardianship under s 5(1)(b) if the deceased mother had a residence order in her favour. In either case, he would have to share parental responsibility with the genetic father, and resolve disputes by seeking an appropriate s 8 order. See Chapter 15 for discussion of s 8 orders.

(c) *If the genetic father is dead, then there is no one with parental responsibility for this child*

   The stepfather can seek a residence order under s 8 or guardianship under s 5(1)(a) Children Act. Guardianship automatically gives him parental responsibility until the child reaches 18 or the court orders otherwise, s 91(7).

4.5.3 Non-relatives

Non-relatives may acquire parental responsibility with a residence order or through guardianship. The principles and comments outlined above in 4.5.2. apply. A local authority obtains parental responsibility for a child under s 31 Children Act, with a care order, sharing it with the child's mother and anyone else who has it. The exercise by others of their parental responsibility in relation to the child may be limited by the local authority under the care order, but there should be partnership and co-operation. The local authority does not acquire parental responsibility when looking after children in voluntary arrangements.

5 Child Protection Procedures in Health and Social Work

Current child protection procedures are set out in *Working Together under the Children Act 1989,* HMSO, 1991 (*Working Together*), the Children Act and the Guidance and Regulations. These mandatory guidelines for local authorities are issued under s 7 of the Local Authority Social Services Act 1970. Non-conformity requires justification.

Social work terminology and practice varies considerably. It is important to know local procedures. The Area Child Protection Committee (ACPC) is a multi-disciplinary group comprising senior representatives from all the child protection agencies and its role is to organise and oversee child protection in its geographical area, producing policy and procedural guidance, published as the ACPC Manual. To obtain a copy, write to the local chair. A small fee to cover costs is usually payable.

5.1 Hierarchy within social services departments

Below is a typical hierarchy of jobs within a social services child protection department. Terminology varies geographically. The head is the **Director of Social Services**, supported by several **Assistant Directors**, each of whom usually has an administrative responsibility related either to an area of work, or a geographical area. Social services departments are generally divided into task related divisions, eg child care, community care, etc. One Assistant Director may have the responsibility for child care, which may or may not include adoption. Out in the field, the front line work is divided into geographical areas, headed by the **Divisional Manager** or **District Manager**. The work is carried out by **social work teams**, usually headed by a **Team Manager**, who is responsible for the management and supervision of the work of the **social workers** in her team.

Figure 5 : Hierarchy within a social services department

SOCIAL SERVICES PERSONNEL CHART
Director of Social Services
Assistant Directors
Divisional Manager or District Manager
Child Protection Officer/Co-Ordinator
Social work teams
Team Manager
Social Workers

5.2 Referral procedures and preliminary investigations

See the flow chart of local authority referral procedures opposite. A member of the public concerned about a child should contact the police or social services. **Police** will usually either use their powers under s 46 Children Act in an emergency, or refer the matter to social services. Social services appoint a **duty officer** for the day in each area. The duty officer will note the information given, ask further details to establish the name, whereabouts and circumstances of the child, and request information about the person making the referral if appropriate. Professionals referring concerns to social services are usually required to confirm the referral in writing within 24 hours. This is to avoid situations where referrals are not properly noted, missed, or for other reasons, not followed up. See para 5.11.1 of *Working Together*. The ACPC must publish contact lists of addresses and telephone numbers. A further safeguard against an inappropriate response or failure to respond to referrals is the **child protection officer.** His role is to oversee and note the progress of the referrals in his area, making sure that they are followed up appropriately and efficiently.

The local authority must decide quickly whether it is necessary to seek emergency protection, child assessment or any other Children Act order. It will immediately trawl for information from the referrer, police, general practitioner, and others to whom the family is known. The

Figure 11: Flow chart of local authority referral procedures

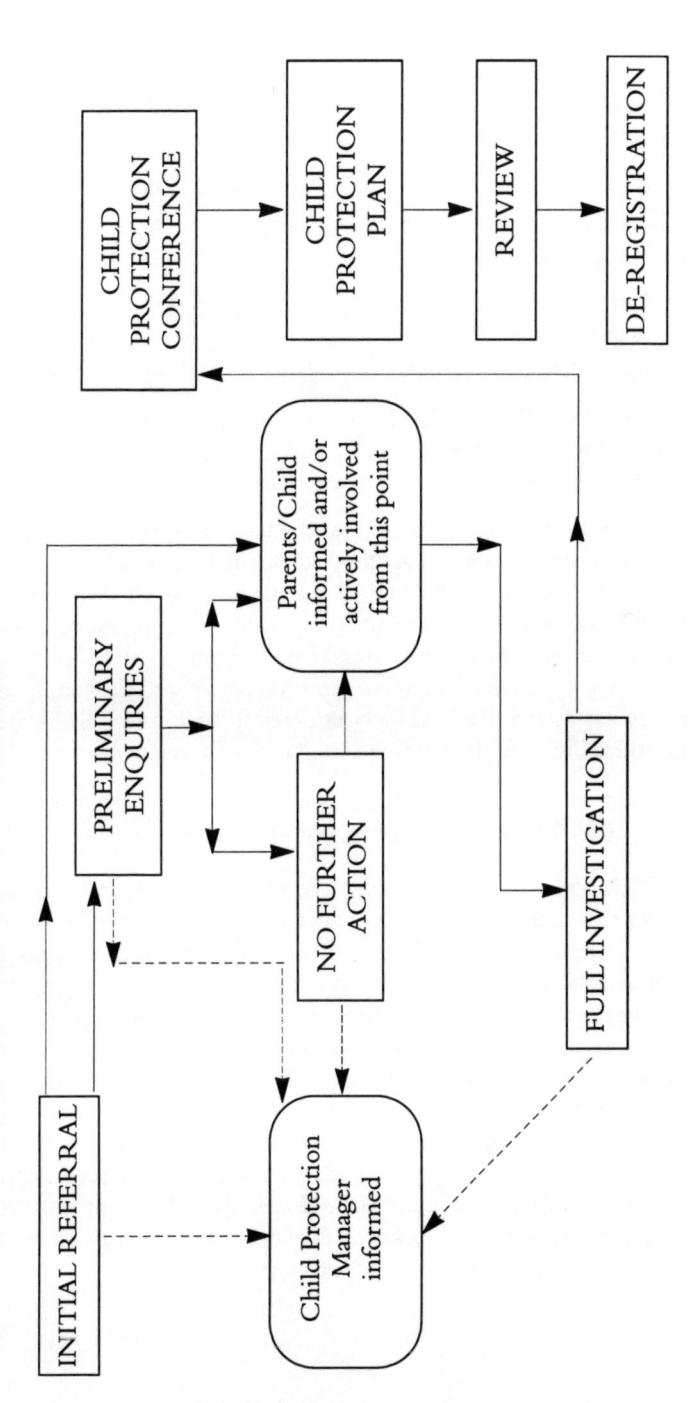

```
INITIAL REFERRAL → PRELIMINARY ENQUIRIES ⇄ Parents/Child informed and/or actively involved from this point
                                         ⇅
                                    NO FURTHER ACTION → Parents/Child informed...
                                         ↓
                                    Child Protection Manager informed
                                         ↓
                                    FULL INVESTIGATION → Parents/Child informed...
                                         ↓
                                    CHILD PROTECTION CONFERENCE → CHILD PROTECTION PLAN → REVIEW → DE-REGISTRATION
```

Note: Court proceedings under the Children Act or Criminal Proceedings may run alongside these Referral and Registration Procedures

Children Act encourages co-operation and negotiation. Parents and carers of children should be told about the referral unless there is a very good reason not to, ie the information would seriously prejudice the safety of the child or a criminal investigation.

Possible outcomes of a preliminary investigation are:
- child protection conference necessary;
- court proceedings;
- Protection can be achieved by working with the parents in negotiation;
- no further action needs to be taken.

Once a decision is reached, the parents, the referrer, those with parental responsibility, and any child of sufficient age and understanding should be informed of the outcome in writing.

Working Together recommends that the letter of information should contain a suitably worded apology acknowledging that whilst a local authority has a statutory duty to investigate referrals, even though the referral was found to be unsubstantiated, the process of investigation is often difficult and painful for everyone involved. It may be necessary for the local authority to offer services to the family, and the investigation needs to be conducted in such a way that it does not interfere with the family's acceptance of service provision.

5.3   Child protection conferences

A Child Protection Conference is a multi-disciplinary discussion about the circumstances of the child held to establish whether the child's name should be placed on the **child protection register**. Registration is followed by the appointment of a social worker (**key worker**) for the family and the formulation of a child protection plan with the agencies involved and the family. A **child protection conference** is not a legal tribunal. It should not allocate blame, generate court action, or assess s 31 criteria for a care application. It has only one decision to make: 'Is registration necessary?' The key worker is not necessarily the person with the most active contact with the family, the title derives from the lead agency, and she fulfils statutory agency responsibilities, including development of the child protection plan, and is lead worker for the inter-agency work.

Figure 6: Function of child protection conference

Decision to be made:

(a) Should child's name be entered on the **child protection register**?

(b) If **yes**, agree date for review – and also appointment of **key worker**

(c) Establish the **core group** of professionals and family

(d) Agree upon the **child protection plan** – see the Family Rights Group model of agreement – and responsibilities of the core group members and family

(e) Agreement on provision of resources for child/family by the local authority

Figure 7: Process of child protection conference

Information gathering
↓
Facts
↓
Opinion
↓
Prognosis for the future
↓
Are the criteria for registration met?
↓
Is there a need for a child protection plan?
↓
Ascertain the view of the conference on registration
↓
Decision

After the child protection conference

Notify those attending of the decision and provide minutes of the conference
↓
Establish the core group
↓
Formulate the child protection plan
↓
Set date for child protection review

Child protection reviews should regularly follow registration at minimum intervals of six months. Extra reviews may be convened at the request of other professionals.

The chair is usually employed by social services, but independent, with no line management responsibility for case work with the family involved. Attendance at child protection conferences is by invitation, which should include all professionals involved with the family, the parents and carers of the child, and the child if of sufficient age and understanding. The chair should ensure that invitees are made welcome, and comfortable, with provision of refreshments, lavatories and other necessities. Minutes should be taken, and decisions recorded. Exclusions should be by the conference chair, and only when justified, eg by a strong risk of violence. The chair is usually assisted by a minute taker, and may call upon specialist advice to assist on racial, ethnic, cultural, legal or religious matters, and psychologists or medical specialists where necessary.

The conference should focus on the needs of the child. Parents and older children may bring with them a supportive adult, whose role is to facilitate their comfort and expression of information and concerns to the conference. They may ask questions for clarification via the chair. Solicitors or legal staff may attend to support a child or parents, but not in an adversarial role, see the Law Society Family Law Committee *Guidance for Solicitors Attending Child Protection Conferences in 1995.*

The provision of resources under s 17 and Sched 2 of the Children Act is a statutory duty for a child in need, see para 5.6 below, and should not depend on registration.

5.4 Child protection register

Grounds for registration

There is, or is a likelihood of, significant harm leading to the need for a **child protection plan** see para 5.5 below.

Either there has been one or more identifiable incidents adversely affecting the child. These could be physical, sexual, emotional or neglectful, and professional judgment is that further incidents are likely.

Or significant harm is expected on the basis of professional judgment of findings of the investigation in this individual case, or on research evidence.

The conference will need to establish as far as it can, the cause of, or likelihood of, the harm. This could apply to other siblings in the same household, justifying their registration. The category must be specified in each child's case.

Figure 8: Categories of abuse for registration

1 **Neglect**

Persistent or severe neglect of a child, failure to protect from danger, extreme failure to carry out aspects of care resulting in impairment of child's health or development, including non-organic failure to thrive.

2 **Physical injury**

Actual or likely physical injury to a child, failure to prevent physical injury or suffering, including deliberate poisoning, suffocation etc and Munchhausen's syndrome by proxy.

3 **Sexual abuse**

Actual or likely sexual exploitation of a child or adolescent. The child may be dependent and/or developmentally immature.

4 **Emotional abuse**

Actual or likely severe adverse effect upon the emotional or behavioural development of a child caused by persistent or severe emotional ill-treatment or rejection. All abuse involves some form of emotional ill-treatment. This category should be used where it is the sole or the main form of the abuse.

Figure 9: Criteria for de-registration

1 **Original factors no longer apply**

This will require a further conference to make the decision to de-register.

2 **Child and/or family moved permanently to another area**

Requirement that the new area has taken over the responsibility for future management of the case.

3 **Child no longer 'child' in the eyes of the law**

If a young person over 16 marries, or when he or she reaches 18, he or she is no longer a 'child' and therefore is not eligible for registration.

4 **The child dies**

5.5 Assessment of risk

Local authorities on referral assess the likelihood of significant harm to a child, ie evaluation of the potential risk to the child should she remain within her family, or the risk to the child if removed from home. After registration there should follow a carefully planned and structured comprehensive assessment within the child protection plan, to gain a better understanding of the child's situation. The Department of Health's *Protecting Children – A Guide for Social Workers Undertaking a Comprehensive Assessment*, HMSO, 1990, referred to colloquially as 'the orange book', is the authoritative reference work, giving questions necessary for a comprehensive assessment. Questions are designed to provide a profile of the family, including physical surroundings and relationships. Social workers are usually given a certain amount of discretion in their use of this assessment model. Buy a copy of the orange book, and use it for reference. Comprehensive assessments require co-operation of agencies and professionals involved with the family. Ask professionals involved about how long they will need, the venue, timing, and personnel to carry out the assessment: all must be clearly agreed.

5.6 Child protection plan

Child protection plans should not be confused with the **care plans** which are required in care proceedings; see para 8.1.

Paragraph 5.17 of *Working Together* recommends that there should be a written plan involving family and professionals. It should in clear language set out the expectations and responsibilities of each party. The Family Rights Group sells a set of blank plan forms, which are approved in *Working Together*. Once the plan is agreed, each person should take responsibility to implement their part of it and to communicate with the others involved, with contingency provisions for crises and regular review. Parents and older children should have a copy of the plan, be informed of the nature and purposes of the interventions offered, and confirm that they agree with the plan and are willing to work with it. If the family have particular preferences about the protection work, which are not accepted by the professionals, then the professionals' reasons should be explained to the family, together with the right of the family to complain or to make representations.

5.7 Local authority duty to promote welfare of children in their area

Section 17 and Sched 2 Children Act 1989 imposes on local authorities a duty to promote the welfare of children in their area, with special provision for 'children in need' (see below para 5.7.2), and children under five years' old. Local authorities must provide family centres as appropriate for children in its area with counselling advice or guidance, occupational, social or recreational activities, Sched 2 para 9(1) Children Act. Local authorities may provide recreational facilities, s 19(1) Local Government (Miscellaneous Provisions) Act 1976. Section 18 Children Act requires provision of day care for children under school age, and for those of school age outside school hours or in the holidays. Section 17(6) Children Act authorises financial help in exceptional circumstances.

5.7.1 Duty to investigate potential or actual harm to child, s 47 Children Act 1989

Section 47 Children Act requires a local authority, when informed that a child who lives or is found in their area is subject to emergency or police protection, or has reasonable cause to suspect that the child is suffering, or is likely to suffer significant harm, to 'make such enquiries as they consider necessary to enable them to decide whether they should take any action to safeguard or promote the child's welfare'.

The enquiries are intended to establish whether the authority should make any application to the court or exercise their powers under the Children Act. The authority should consider providing accommodation for a child subject to an emergency protection order if they are not already doing so, s 47(3)(b); and if the child is in police protection, then the authority should consider applying for an emergency protection order, s 47(3)(c). Enquiries include schooling. Refusal of access to the child or denial of information justifies an application for an emergency protection order. The local authority is under a duty to consider and timetable a review, if no present action is required. If action is necessary then the authority is under a duty to take it, s 47(8).

5.7.2 Duty to children in need

Section 17(1) Children Act imposes on local authorities a twofold duty: '(a) to safeguard and promote the welfare of children within their area who are in need and (b) ... to promote the upbringing of such children by their families, by providing a range and level of services appropriate to those children's needs.' Under s 17, those services are free to families on income support or family credit, but otherwise may be subject to means-related contributions.

Section 17(10) defines a child being in need if '(a) he is unlikely to achieve or maintain, or to have the opportunity of achieving or maintaining, a reasonable standard of health or development without the provision for him of services by the local authority ... (b) his health or development is likely to be significantly impaired, or further impaired, without the provision for him of such services; or (c) he is disabled'. The services can be provided to the child direct, or to the family for the benefit of the child. Local authorities should publish information about the services in their area, Sched 2 para 1(2)(a)(i) Children Act. The types of service which should be provided are listed, see Fig 5.

'Health', 'development' and 'disabled' are all defined in the Children Act. The term 'disabled' was adopted to conform with the wording of the National Assistance Act 1948. Under s 17(6) Children Act assistance may be financial in exceptional circumstances, or in kind.

Figure 10: Services for children and families

Schedule 2 para 8 Children Act 1989:
- advice guidance and counselling;
- occupational, social, cultural or recreational activities;
- home help (which may include laundry facilities);
- facilities for, or assistance with travelling to and from home for the purpose of taking advantage of any other service provided under this Act or similar service;
- assistance to enable the child concerned and his family to have a holiday.

5.7.3 Duty to children under five

There is power under s 18 Children Act to provide day care for children under school age. *The Children Act 1989 Guidance and Regulations* Vol 2, 'Family Support, Day Care and Educational Provision for Young

Children' is helpful in giving ideas to practitioners about the nature and standards of the provision to be expected.

5.7.4 Compliance with court order to investigate child's circumstances, s 37 Children Act 1989

Under s 37 Children Act in any 'family proceedings' in which a question arises as to the welfare of any child, if it appears to the court that it may be appropriate for a care or supervision order to be made, the court may order the local authority to investigate the child's circumstances. The local authority then has to consider whether they should: apply for a care or supervision order, provide services for the family, or take any other action with respect to the child, s 37(2). If they decide not to seek an order, their reasons must be reported to the court within eight weeks, as must the services provided or to be provided, and any other action taken or proposed with respect to the child, s 37(3) and (4). The local authority may also need to review the situation and set a date for such a review, s 37(6). The Children Act Advisory Committee recognises the need for clear guidance as to the use by the courts of s 37, and the reasons and information to be supplied on the making of an order. Guidance is also needed on the role of Guardians *ad litem* in cases where s 37 directions are made, and on the distinction between the use of s 7 directions for a court welfare report and s 37. Directions and guidance should be issued in the near future on these issues.

6 Emergency Protection Orders

Emergency protection orders made under s 44 Children Act 1989 (the 'Children Act') are designed for situations when a child needs to be removed to a safe place, or once there to be kept in a safe place, such as a hospital. They are also useful where there is no access to a child in danger, and urgent action is necessary. An order may be made in respect of any child under 18 years of age living or found within the jurisdiction of the court.

6.1 Effects of order

The order gives parental responsibility for the child to the applicant, s 44(5). It authorises the applicant to remove, or retain the child, s 44(4)(b); and operates as a direction to anyone in a position to do so, to produce the child, s 44(4)(a). Under s 44(15) it is a criminal offence to obstruct the applicant in the exercise of his powers under the order.

The order has wide powers, and may contain any or all of these directions:

- Authorising doctor, nurse, or health visitor to accompany the applicant to carry out the order, s 45(12) Children Act.
- For child to have contact with any named person, s 44(6)(a).
- For medical or psychiatric examination of the child, s 44(6)(b).
- Requirement to disclose information concerning whereabouts of the child, s 48(1).
- Authorisation to enter premises and search for the child, s 48(3).
- Authorisation to search for another child in the same premises, s 48(4).
- Issue of warrant to police officer to assist the applicant, s 48(9).
- Authorisation for nurse, doctor, or health visitor to accompany police, s 48(11).

6.2 Duration

Emergency protection orders last initially for eight days, renewable for a further seven days, s 45(1).

There are some exceptions to this general rule:
- if order would expire on public holiday – first order goes to noon on the next day, s 45(2);
- if child in police protection (duration 76 hours maximum) before emergency protection order, and the designated police officer is the applicant on behalf of the local authority, the emergency protection order commences from beginning of police protection, s 45(3).

6.3 Grounds for application

The grounds to be proved depend upon who the applicant is.

Since anyone can apply for this order there is a general ground.

If the intention is to remove a child to a safe place, the applicant must satisfy the court that there is reasonable cause to believe that the child will suffer significant harm if not removed to accommodation provided by him, and also that there is suitable accommodation available for the child, s 44(1)(a)(i) Children Act. If the applicant intends to retain the child in a safe place, then it must be proved that the applicant has reasonable cause to believe that the child is likely to suffer significant harm unless retained, s 44(1)(a)(ii). The grounds can be on a prognosis, or based on past events to assess future risk to the child. For the meaning of 'significant harm' see Chapter 8 at 8.4 below.

A local authority applicant has an additional ground. It can satisfy the court that during s 47 Children Act enquiries about a child in its area, access to the child requested by a person authorised to seek it is being refused unreasonably, and that the access is required as a matter of urgency, s 44(1)(b)(ii) Children Act. See Chapter 5 at 5.6.1 for s 47 investigations. The question of reasonable refusal is a matter for the court. The Children Act 1989 Guidance Vol 1 'Court Orders' at para 4.39 gives examples either way.

If the application is by an 'authorised person' (currently only the NSPCC), there is either the general ground, or an additional ground, that the applicant has reasonable cause to suspect that the child is suffering or is likely to suffer significant harm, that the applicant is making enquiries as to the child's welfare, that access to the child is being unreasonably refused, and access is urgently needed, s 44(1) Children Act.

6.4 Practice and procedure

6.4.1 Application

Emergency protection orders may be sought by any person. Usually, the applicant is an 'authorised officer' of the local authority, or 'a designated officer' of the police.

The application should be made in the family proceedings court, unless the local authority has been directed to investigate under s 37, or there are proceedings pending in another court. In these exceptional cases the application can be made in the relevant court, Children (Allocation of Proceedings) Order 1991 art 3. Application is on form C1, together with form C11. Procedure is governed by Sched 1 Family Proceedings Courts (Children Act 1989) Rules 1991 (FPC (CA) R 1991) and App 1 Family Proceedings Rules 1991 (FPR 1991) and r 4.4(4)(a). Applications for extensions should be made to the court which made the original order, art 4. The application should name the child, and if this is not possible, it should give a description of the child for identification purposes.

A guardian *ad litem* will be appointed by the court to oversee the welfare of the child and to advise the court on the child's best interests, see ss 41–42 Children Act, and Chapter 16 below para 16.1

6.4.2 Notice

Application may be made *ex parte*, but first, in the family proceedings court, the leave of the justice's clerk or a magistrate must be obtained, r 4(4)(a) FPC (CA) R 1991 and r 4.4(4)(a) FPR 1991.

Notice of the proceedings on form C6A, and the date, time and venue of the application must be given within one day of the hearing to:
- parents without parental responsibility for the child;
- any person caring for the child or with whom the child is living;
- a local authority providing accommodation for the child;
- a person providing a refuge in which child lives.

See r 4(1)(b) and Sched 2 col (iv) FPC (CA) R 1991; r 4.4(1)(b) and App 3 col (iv) FPR 1991.

6.4.3 Respondents

The forms of notice plus a copy of the application must be served on those listed below who are automatic respondents to the application:
- everyone with parental responsibility for the child;
- if there is a care order, all those who had parental responsibility immediately prior to the care order;
- the child if of sufficient age and understanding.

See r 7(1) Sched 2 col (iii) FPC (CA) R 1991 and r 4.7(1) App 3 col (iii) FPR 1991. Others may be joined as respondents, and automatic respondents may be removed.

6.4.4 Service

Service must be effected one day before the directions or application hearing, r 4.4(1)(b) Sched 2 FPC (CA) R 1991 and r 4.4.4.(1)(b) App 3 FPR 1991.

6.4.5 Attendance

By r 16(2) FPC (CA) R 1991 and r 4.16.2 FPR 1991, the parties and/or their legal representatives have to attend directions appointments and hearings unless otherwise directed by the court. If respondents fail to appear, the court may proceed in their absence. If applicants fail to attend the court may refuse their application, r 16(5) and r 4.16(5).

The Children Act principles of the paramountcy of the welfare of the child, avoidance of delay and no order unless necessary for the welfare of the child apply, but the application is not 'family proceedings' within the meaning of s 8(4) Children Act and so the 'welfare checklist' does not apply.

6.5 Contact, accommodation and the rights of the child

6.5.1 Contact

The child must be allowed reasonable contact with:
- parents;
- those with parental responsibility for the child;
- anyone with whom the child was living before the order;

- anyone with a contact order under s 8 or s 34 in force in respect of the child, or anyone acting on their behalf;
- anyone with an order for access to the child, s 44(13) Children Act.

The court can control the contact by directions within the emergency protection order. See s 44(13)(dd), s 44(6)(a) and Sched 14 para 9(4) Children Act.

Principles and Practice in Guidance, paras 14-16 are relevant to contact issues, see also *Guidance and Regulations* Volume 4 'Residential Care' ('Residential Care') at paras 2-5 to 2-6.

6.5.2 Accommodation

The child has the right to accommodation provided, funded, or arranged by the local authority and which meets the standards set by Residential Care, by the Arrangements for Placement of Children Regulations 1991, and by Sched 2 Children Act.

6.5.3 Rights of the child

The child has the right to be returned to his home once the danger has passed and the grounds for the order no longer subsist, s 44(10) Children Act.

A child of sufficient age and understanding has the right to be consulted and informed about events that are happening, see *Residential Care* at paras 2.20(c); 2.21; and 2.10-2.12.

The emergency protection order may include a direction about medical or psychiatric assessment of the child, s 44 Children Act. The directions can order or prohibit examinations, either completely or without leave of the court. Directions for examination/assessment can include venue, personnel to be present, and nomination of the person(s) to whom results should be given. A child of sufficient age and understanding has the right to make an informed refusal of medical or psychiatric assessment. A '*Gillick* competent' child, or a young person over 16 may consent to or refuse medical treatment, see Chapter 13 below at 13.1 and 13.2.

6.6 Variation and discharge

There is no appeal against an emergency protection order, perhaps because of its short duration. It can be challenged by an application to vary or to discharge the order.

The child, child's parents, those with parental responsibility for the child, and anyone with whom the child was living when the order was made can make an application for variation or discharge, s 45(8) Children Act.

The rules provide, however, that if a person has had notice of the original application for the emergency protection order, and has attended and opposed the application at the hearing, then there is no right to seek a discharge, s 45(11) Children Act . There has to be a time lapse of 72 hours after the order is made before there can be a hearing of an application for discharge, s 45(9) Children Act.

7 Child Assessment Orders

7.1 Effects of order

Child assessment orders were created by s 43 Children Act 1989 ('Children Act'). Vol 1 *Children Act 1989 Guidance and Regulations* 'Court Orders' ('Court Orders') makes it clear in para 4.11 that a child assessment order application should follow on from a s 47 investigation (see 5.6.1 above). It enables the local authority to discover sufficient information about the child to plan appropriate action in the child's interests. Paragraph 4.9 Court Orders considers this order appropriate 'where the harm to the child is long-term and cumulative rather than sudden and severe'. It is appropriate where there is no emergency necessitating removal of a child from home for protection, but the parents or carers of the child are demonstrably failing to co-operate with the local authority in facilitating an assessment. The order can stipulate the nature of the assessment sought, the venue and duration, the person(s) to whom the results are to be given, and the contact between the child and others during the subsistence of the order.

7.2 Grounds for application

The court may by s 43(1) Children Act make the order only if it is satisfied that:

(a) the applicant has reasonable cause to suspect that the child is suffering, or is likely to suffer significant harm;

(b) an assessment of the child's state of health or development, or of the way in which he is being treated, is required to enable the applicant to determine whether or not the child is suffering or is likely to suffer significant harm; and

(c) it is unlikely that such an assessment will be made, or be satisfactory, in the absence of an order under this section.

7.3 Practice and procedure

7.3.1 Application

Application can only be made by a local authority or authorised officer (NSPCC), see s 43(1) and (13) and s 31(9) Children Act. It should be on form C1 together with form C16. It must be determined at a full court hearing.

7.3.2 Venue

Under the Children (Allocation of Proceedings) Order 1991 SI 1991/1677 the application should be made in the family proceedings court, unless there are pending proceedings in another court, or the application is the result of a court direction to investigate under s 37 (see 5.6.4 above).

7.3.3 Notice

Notice of the proceedings on form C6A, and the date, time and venue of the application must be given to:
- parents;
- those with parental responsibility for the child;
- any person caring for the child or with whom the child is living;
- anyone with a contact order under s 8 or s 34 Children Act 1989, (or former access order);
- local authority providing accommodation for the child;
- person providing a refuge in which child lives;
- the child, if of sufficient age and understanding.

Rule 4(3) FPC (CA) R 1991 Sched 1 and Sched 2 col (iv) and FPR 1991 r 4.4(3) and App 3 col (iv).

7.3.4 Respondents

The forms of notice plus a copy of the application must be served on those listed below who are automatic respondents to the application:
- everyone with parental responsibility for the child;
- the child if of sufficient age and understanding;
- where there is a care order, everyone with parental responsibility before the making of the care order. See Sched 2 col (iii) FPC(CA) 1991 and App 3 col (iii) FPR 1991.

Others may be joined as respondents, and automatic respondents may be removed. Rule 7(1) FPC (CA) 1991 and r 4.7(1) FPR 1991.

7.3.5 Service

Service must be seven days before the directions or application hearing. Rule 4.4(1)(b) Sched 2 FPC (CA) 1991 and App 3 FPR 1991.

7.3.6 Generally

Section 1 Children Act principles (see Chapter 3 above) apply to s 43 applications.

The duration of the order is limited to seven days from the date specified for commencement, s 43(5). The Act does not state that the seven days must be consecutive, but there seems no other practicable interpretation. It cannot be extended, and unless the court grants leave, it cannot be renewed until a six month period has elapsed, s 91(15) Children Act.

Section 8(4)(a) Children Act defines 'family proceedings', and within these proceedings the court has power to make other orders of its own volition. Section 43 orders are not 'family proceedings'. This means that the court can only make or refuse the order sought, or treat the application as one for an emergency protection order instead, s 43(3). The court must not make a child assessment order if in all the circumstances of the case the court considers an emergency protection order more appropriate, s 43(4).

7.3.7 Discharge of order

On an application for discharge of a child assessment order the case will be listed for directions. The procedure is the same as an application for an original order.

7.4 Contact, accommodation and the rights of the child

7.4.1 Contact

There are no specific rules as to contact, but it is submitted that the comments in *Principles and Practice in Guidance*, paras 14–16 and *Guidance and Regulations* Vol 4 'Residential Care' ('Residential Care') at paras 2-5 to 2-6 relevant to contact with a child in care are applicable to this

situation. This would mean that the child should be allowed reasonable contact with:
- parents;
- those with parental responsibility for the child;
- anyone with whom the child was living before the order;
- anyone with a contact order under s 8 or s 34 in force in respect of the child, or anyone acting on their behalf;
- anyone with an order for access to the child, s 44(13) Children Act.

The court can control contact by directions within the child assessment order.

See s 43(10) Children Act.

7.4.2 Accommodation

The child has the right, if removed from home, to reside in accommodation provided, funded, or arranged by the local authority which meets the standards set by *Residential Care*, by the Arrangements for Placement of Children Regulations 1991, and by Sched 2 Children Act.

7.4.3 Rights of the child

A child of sufficient age and understanding has the right to be consulted and informed about events that are happening, see *Residential Care* at paras 2.20(c); 2.21; and 2.10-2.12.

The child assessment order will usually include a direction about medical or psychiatric assessment of the child. Examinations can be ordered or prohibited. Directions can include venue, personnel to be present, and nomination of the person(s) to whom results of assessments etc should be given. A child of sufficient age and understanding has the right to make an informed refusal of medical or psychiatric assessment, s 43(8) Children Act . A '*Gillick* competent' child, or a young person over 16 may consent to or refuse medical treatment, see Chapter 13 below paras 13.1 and 13.2.

7.5   Appeals, variation and discharge

Appeal lies against the making or refusal of a child assessment order, from the family proceedings court to the High Court, and from the county court or High Court to the Court of Appeal, see Chapter 17 below.

Applications to vary or discharge the order may be made on form C1, with two days' notice, to the court which made the original order, art 4, Children (Allocation of Proceedings) Order 1991.

8 Care and Supervision Proceedings

8.1 Effects

Care orders are made under s 31 Children Act 1989 ('Children Act') placing a child into the care of a local authority. A child is a person under the age of 18, s 105(1). Care order includes an interim order under s 38. Reference to a 'child in care', means a child subject to a care order, and not a child looked after by the local authority under a voluntary arrangement.

A care order cannot be made in respect of a child over 17 years old, or 16 if married, s 31(3) Children Act.

There is only one route into statutory care. The court must be satisfied of the criteria set out in s 31 Children Act, and that an order is necessary for the welfare of the child.

The underlying principles in s 1(1), (2) and (5) Children Act – the paramountcy of the welfare of the child, avoidance of delay and no order unless necessary – all apply. The court must have regard to the welfare checklist in s 1(3), see Chapter 3.

8.2 Grounds for application for a care or supervision order

Section 31(1) Children Act specifies the grounds for application for a care or supervision order:

(a) that the child concerned is suffering or likely to suffer significant harm; and

(b) that the harm; or likelihood of harm, is attributable to:

(i) the care given to the child, or likely to be given to him if an order were not made, not being what it would be reasonable to expect a parent to give to him; or

(ii) the child's being beyond parental control.

- *Harm* is defined in s 31(9) Children Act as 'ill treatment or the impairment of health or development'.
- *Development* means physical, intellectual, emotional, social or behavioural development.
- *Health* includes physical or mental health.
- *Ill treatment* includes sexual abuse and forms of ill treatment which are not physical.

Significant harm must be attributable to parental care falling below a reasonable standard, or the child being beyond parental control. The test is objective, measured against a reasonable standard of parenting.

In *Re M (Minor) (Care Order)* [1994] 3 All ER 298 HL; [1994] 2 AC 424; [1994] 3 WLR 558; [1994] 2 FLR 577 the court held that 'is suffering' means at the date of the hearing, or at the moment when the child was initially protected, provided the protection is uninterrupted until the date of the hearing. A careful reading of this judgment is recommended. The court may consider circumstances prevailing at the hearing date in considering the most appropriate order.

8.2.1 Standard of proof

Significant harm must be established on a balance of probabilities. In *Re P (Minor) (Care Proceedings)* [1995] 1 FCR 583 the court held that the more serious the allegation, the more convincing the evidence needed to tip the balance.

In *Re H and R (Minors)(Sexual abuse: standard of proof)* [1996] 1 FCR 509 the application was for a care order in respect of four children, based on an allegation of sexual abuse of the oldest child by the father, and therefore a likelihood of significant harm to the younger three. The House of Lords confirmed that the s 31(2) criteria was not met in the case of the oldest child, leaving no power to go on and consider the likelihood of harm to the younger three children.

8.3 Practice and procedure

8.3.1 Application

Only a local authority or authorised person may apply for a care order, s 31(1) Children Act. An 'authorised person' at the moment is an officer of the NSPCC, s 31(9). Applications should be made in the family proceedings court, unless one of three exceptions apply: there has been a court directed investigation under s 37 Children Act 1989; there are pending proceedings; or the application is to extend, vary or discharge an existing order. In these exceptional cases, the application may be made in the same court as the other proceedings, art 3, Children (Allocation of Proceedings) Order 1991. County courts are divided into divorce centres, care centres and family hearing centres. Care and supervision applications must be heard in care centres. Refer to the Family Proceedings (Allocation to Judiciary) Directions 1993 [1993] 2 FLR 1008. Transfers are governed by the Children (Allocation of Proceedings) Order 1991, SI 1991/1677; and the Children (Allocation of Proceedings, Appeals) Order 1991, SI 1991/1801 and the Family Proceedings (Amendment) Rules 1991, SI 1991/2113; also Home Office Circular 45/91.

Here there is space only to summarise these provisions, and to draw attention to potential pitfalls which may be encountered. Under art 21 Children (Allocation of Proceedings) Order 1991, if the procedural requirements are broken, proceedings are not invalidated nor is it ground for appeal.

Examples of cases which should be heard in the High Court are:
- post-adoption contact applications;
- specific issue – blood transfusions;
- HIV test for a child;
- injunctions concerning publicity;
- applications by a child for leave to apply for a s 8 order.

See the *Practice Direction* [1993] 1 WLR 313 and 1 All ER 820.

Figure 12: Transfer 'trigger list'

The Children Act Advisory Committee has suggested that the presence of one of the factors listed below may give rise to transfer; the presence of two factors is rather more persuasive, and the presence of three or more trigger factors should lead to a transfer.

Cases which cannot be heard on consecutive days

Analysis of conflicting expert evidence

Evaluation of psychiatric or medical evidence or allied professional evidence

Ritual or multiple sexual abuse

Issues affecting recently-born babies

Multiplicity of children or parties

Involvement of more than one local authority

Confidential material evidence

Cases likely to last longer than two or three days

Where delay would occur unless transferred

Termination of contact

Conflict between GAL and child

Novel issues or facts

Conflict between protocols

Any other circumstance which makes case suitable for higher court

Application by a child

(Section 8 applications by a child must be heard in the High Court)

8.3.2 Notice

Notice on form C6A, with the date, time and venue of the application must be served three days before the hearing on:
- parents without parental responsibility for the child;
- any person caring for the child or with whom the child is living;
- a local authority providing accommodation for the child;
- a person providing a refuge in which child lives;
- any person who is party to relevant proceedings in respect of the child.

See r 4(3) FPC (CA) R 1991 Sched 1 and Sched 2 col (iv) and FPR 1991 r 4.4(3) and App 3 col (iv).

8.3.3 Respondents

The forms of notice plus a copy of the application must be served on those listed below who are automatic respondents to the application:
- everyone with parental responsibility for the child;
- the child if of sufficient age and understanding.

See r 7(1) Sched 2 col (iii) FPC (CA) 1991 and r 4.7(1) App 3 col (iii) FPR 1991. Others may be joined as respondents, and automatic respondents may be removed.

8.3.4 Service

Service must be three days before the directions or application hearing, r 4.4(1)(b) Sched 2 FPC (CA) 1991 and App 3 FPR 1991. The court can dispense with the requirements of service *Re X (Care: Notice of Proceedings)* [1996] 1 FLR 186. The welfare principle does not apply in consideration of service since it is not a substantive application.

8.3.5 Attendance

Proceedings must take place in the child's absence if the court considers this in his interests, having regard to the matters to be discussed or the evidence likely to be given, and he is represented by a solicitor, r 16(2) FPC (CA) R 1991 and r 4.16.2, FPR 1991.

By the same rule, the other parties and/or their legal representatives have to attend directions appointments and hearings unless otherwise directed by the court. If respondents fail to appear, the court may proceed in their absence. If applicants fail to attend the court may refuse their application, r 16(5) and r 4.16(5).

Directions hearings are used by the court to oversee the timing of the case, the filing and service of evidence, and the appointment of parties and the guardian ad litem. For discussion of the use of directions hearings and case preparation see Chapter 12 below.

8.4 Significant harm

The difficult part for practitioners in care and supervision proceedings is often the definition of 'significant harm'. Section 31(9) Children Act defines 'harm' as the impairment of health or development; 'development' means physical, intellectual, emotional, social or behavioural development; 'health' means mental or physical health; and 'ill treatment' includes sexual abuse and forms of ill treatment which are not physical. It is also provided in s 31(10) that: 'Where the question of whether harm suffered by a child is significant turns upon the child's health or development, his health or development shall be compared with that which could reasonably be expected of a similar child.' The court will therefore have to compare this particular child with a notional similar child, of similar background, age, ethnicity, culture, race, religion and physique.

Significant Harm by M Adcock, R White and A Hollows, Significant Publications, London 1991, gives useful information from a variety of medical and psychological perspectives about the assessment of harm. Richard White leads the reader step by step through a logical process of evaluating whether the successive stages of the threshold criteria are met. It helps in case preparation and effective evidence gathering, and assists in explaining the criteria to the court. (See figure 13, p 65.)

8.5 Interim orders

On adjourning a care or supervision application, the court has the power to make an interim order when satisfied that there are reasonable grounds for believing the circumstances justifying a care order exist, s 38(2) Children Act. An interim order's maximum duration is an initial maximum of eight weeks, followed by extensions of up to four weeks each. Shorter interim orders are possible, s 38(4) and (5) Children Act.

Figure 13: Significant harm flow chart

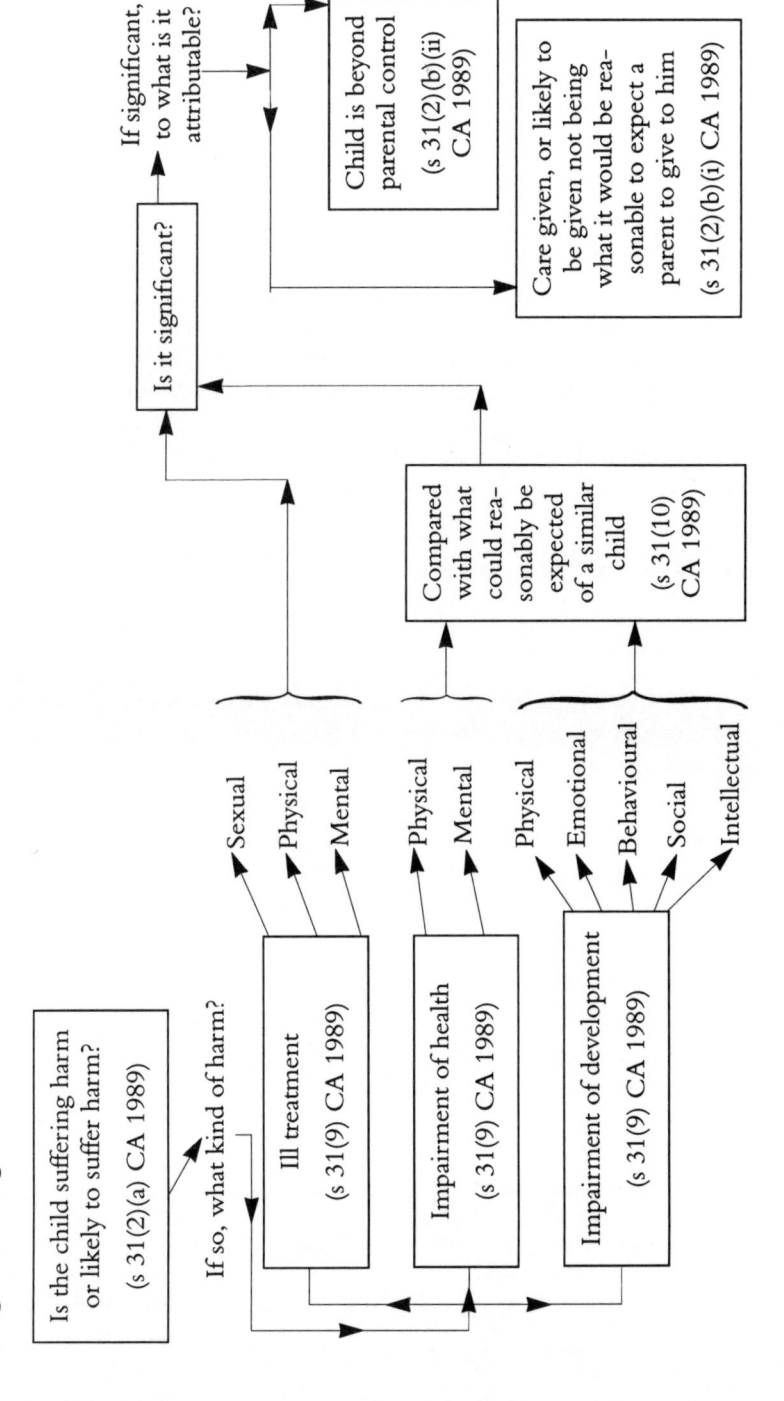

Is the child suffering harm or likely to suffer harm? (s 31(2)(a) CA 1989)

If so, what kind of harm?

- **Ill treatment** (s 31(9) CA 1989) — Sexual, Physical, Mental
- **Impairment of health** (s 31(9) CA 1989) — Physical, Mental
- **Impairment of development** (s 31(9) CA 1989) — Physical, Emotional, Behavioural, Social, Intellectual

Compared with what could reasonably be expected of a similar child (s 31(10) CA 1989)

Is it significant?

If significant, to what is it attributable?

- Child is beyond parental control (s 31(2)(b)(ii) CA 1989)
- Care given, or likely to be given not being what it would be reasonable to expect a parent to give to him (s 31(2)(b)(i) CA 1989)

- The *initial interim* order may be up to eight weeks.
- If the initial order is less than eight weeks, then the *second interim* order must be no more than a total of eight weeks less the duration of the initial interim order (eg first order: five weeks, second: three; or first order: two weeks, second: six).
- Any *subsequent orders* must be of no more than four weeks' duration.

The Act seeks to avoid delay in dealing with cases. Courts will not permit repeated interim orders.

On making an interim order, directions may require medical or psychiatric examination/assessment of the child, which a child of sufficient understanding may refuse, s 38(6) Children Act. See Chapter 13 below for the rights of children. Directions may also prevent the abuse of children by repeated examinations, s 38(7) Children Act. Directions may also govern the time and venue of the examination, who shall be present, and to whom the results will be given.

8.6 Effects of care order

8.6.1 Duration

A care order subsists until the child reaches 18, unless brought to an end earlier by the court, s 91(1) and (12) Children Act. It will cease on the making of:

- an adoption or a freeing order, Adoption Act 1976 ss 12(3) and 18(5);
- a residence order, s 91(1) Children Act;
- the making of a supervision order in substitution for a care order, s 39(4) Children Act;
- the making of an order for discharge of care, s 39(1) Children Act;
- if the child goes to live in Northern Ireland, the Channel islands or the Isle of Man then the order may cease to be enforceable but the regulations about this have not yet been made under s 101(4) Children Act.

8.6.2 Parental responsibility

The local authority acquires parental responsibility under a care order, sharing it with those who already have it. It may, however, limit the exercise of parental responsibility by others whilst the care order subsists, s 33(3) Children Act. There are limits on the powers of the local authority during a care order. They may not change a child's religion; consent to his adoption; or appoint a guardian for the child, s 33. The parental responsibility which others had when the care order was made still subsists, but it cannot be exercised in a way which conflicts with a court order, s 2(6) and (8) Children Act. The child's name may not be changed or the child removed from the United Kingdom without written consent of all with parental responsibility or leave of the court, s 33(7). The local authority may remove the child from the jurisdiction of the court for up to one month, and under Sched 2 para 19, Children Act, the local authority can make arrangements for a child to live abroad, with certain restrictions.

8.6.3 Accommodation of the child

Under s 33(1) Children Act, the local authority has a duty to receive the child into its care once the order is made. The child is the responsibility of the local authority, and it must provide for somewhere to live and maintenance for the child, s 23(1) Children Act. The child may remain at home. The Guidance Vol 4 'Residential Care' and Vol 3 'Family Placements' govern the placements of children in residential and foster care, and placements with their family. There is a duty on the local authority to keep children with their birth family if at all possible, consistent with their welfare, and 'Principles and Practice in Regulations and Guidance' paras 5, 8, 9, and 10 emphasise the importance of maintaining family links, and of the primary duty to try to keep a child at home by the provision of resources. A care order and removal of a child is seen as the last resort, and in itself 'a risk to be balanced against others', para 8.

8.6.4 Contact with a child in care

Paragraphs 2.6 and 6.26, Vol 4 of the *Guidance* 'Residential Placements' assume that contact with its family is in the best interests of a child in care unless proved otherwise. Parents and others in financial or practical difficulty should receive help with travelling to contact sessions, Sched 2 para 16 Children Act.

Contact with children in care is subject to the control of the court. This is different from contact in private law, and orders available under s 34 Children Act are referred to as 'care contact orders'. The Act requires that children looked after by a local authority under a care order will be afforded 'reasonable contact' with those people listed in s 34(1). They are:

- parents;
- guardians;
- anyone with a residence order in force immediately before the care order was made;
- anyone with care of the child under a High Court order made under its inherent jurisdiction.

The court may, on the application of the guardian *ad litem* or the child, make whatever order it considers appropriate in respect of contact between the child and any named person. Where the child or the local authority is the applicant, the scope of the order is very wide. On the application of any person entitled to contact under s 34(1) (those listed above), or anyone else with leave of the court, a care contact order may be made.

When the court makes a care order, it may make a care contact order if necessary in the interests of the child, s 34(5) Children Act. The forms, those entitled to notice and respondents, are the same as for the care order, save that the period of notice is three days, see r 4(1)(b) FPC (CA) R 1991 and FPR 1991 r 4.4(1)(b).

In urgent cases, if necessary, a local authority may stop contact for up to seven days, s 34(6) Children Act. If it wishes to stop contact for longer, it must apply to the court for a care contact order under s 34, authorising contact with a named person to be curtailed or to be refused. It is argued that severe curtailment of contact is tantamount to a refusal within the meaning of s 34 since the section refers to 'reasonable contact' and the court is the ultimate arbiter of reasonableness.

8.6.5 Rights of the child in care proceedings and under a care order

A child in care has rights which are protected by the Children Act 1989 and also by the guidance issued under it. The child has a right to:

- refuse medical or psychiatric assessment ordered within an interim care order under s 38(6) Children Act;
- contact with his or her family, see 8.6.4 above, and 'Principles and Practice' in *Guidance* paras 9 and 13-16 (see 'Sources' at 1.1.5 above);
- consultation on issues involving her care, see *Guidance* Vol 3 para 2.21 and para 6.4; also *Guidance* Vol 4 paras 2.21 and 2.45; ss 22(4), 61 and 64 Children Act; para 25 'Principles and Practice' in *Guidance*;
- information about issues involving his care;
- have her wishes and feelings taken into account, ss 22(4), 61 and 64 Children Act, 'Principles and Practice' in *Guidance* para 25;

- have his race, culture, religion and background taken into account in care proceedings, s 1 Children Act and para 4 'Principles and Practice' in *Guidance*;
- consult a solicitor of her own if of sufficient age and understanding;
- develop a sense of identity, para 19 'Principles and Practice' in *Guidance*;
- grow to independence, para 26 'Principles and Practice' in Guidance;
- to live in peace and safety, free from abuse, para 3 'Principles and Practice' in *Guidance*.

8.6.6 Rights of parents of a child in care

'Principles and Practice' in *Guidance* establish the rights of parents and children.

Parents (with parental responsibility or not), and those with parental responsibility for a child in care, have the right to:

- consultation when plans are being made, para 2.53 Guidance Vol 4, paras 7 and 10 'Principles and Practice' in *Guidance*;
- information on where their child is being kept, Sched 2 para 15(2) Children Act;
- reasonable contact with their child s 34 Children Act, paras 14-16, 'Principles and Practice' in *Guidance*;
- receive financial or practical assistance with travelling to see their child Sched 2 para 16;
- be a party to written agreements about the child's placement *Guidance* Vol 4 para 2.63;
- participate actively in planning for the child's future, *Guidance* Vol 4 para 2.49.

Para 2.49, Vol 4 of the *Guidance* states: 'The child's family, parents, grandparents, and other relatives involved with the child should be invited to participate actively in planning and to make their views known.'

8.7 Effects of supervision order

Supervision orders place children under the supervision of a local authority or a probation officer. The duties and powers of the supervising officer are set out in s 35 and Sched 3 Children Act, including a duty 'to advise, assist and befriend' the child. The sanction for non-cooperation is application to discharge the order and to substitute something else, possibly a care order, see 8.7.3 below. Directions may be made within supervision orders binding those responsible for the child and also the child to attend activities or live at specified places, see 8.7.2 below. They subsist for the duration of the supervision order or such lesser period as the court may specify.

A supervision order is possible within criminal proceedings on a finding of guilt against a juvenile offender. Those orders can contain a direction that a child lives in local authority accommodation for a period of up to six months. However, the criteria in s 31 Children Act do not have to be met before a 'criminal supervision order' is made. Criminal supervision orders are not discussed in this book, because they are different from orders made under s 31 Children Act. However, a child in local authority accommodation under a criminal supervision order must have the same rights under Vol 4 of the *Guidance* 'Residential Care' as a child living away from home under a Children Act care or supervision order.

8.7.1 Duration

If a care or supervision application is adjourned, the court can make an interim order, s 38(1) Children Act. Section 38(3) provides that if there is an application for care, but the court decides to make a residence order (for limited duration) instead of a care order, then the court must also make an interim supervision order unless it is satisfied that the child's welfare will be adequately safeguarded without one.

A supervision order can last for up to one year, s 91(3) and Sched 3 para 6 Children Act. It may be for shorter duration if ordered by the court. A supervision order may also be extended for a further period or periods up to a maximum of three years from the date it was first made, Sched 3 para 6(3) and (4) Children Act. Section 1 Children Act 1989 principles apply (see Chapter 3 above).

8.7.2 Directions

Directions to the child

The court may embody in the order a general term along the lines that 'the child must comply with the directions of the supervisor'. The supervisor then has a certain amount of leeway about the directions given, provided they fall within the parameters set in Sched 3 para 2 Children Act.

These are:
- to live at a place or places specified;
- to present himself to a person or persons specified for a period or periods specified;
- to participate in specified activities on dates and at times specified.

Directions to a 'responsible person'

A responsible person is defined in Sched 3 para 1 Children Act as 'a person who has parental responsibility for the child, and any other person with whom the child is living.'

Under Sched 3, with the consent of the responsible person, the court can include in the order a number of requirements:
- to take reasonable steps to ensure the child complies with the directions of the supervisor to live at a specified place, present himself to a person specified on a specific day, and to participate in activities;
- to take all reasonable steps to ensure the supervised child complies with directions regarding medical and psychiatric examinations;
- that he comply with direction of supervisor 'to attend at [the] place specified in the directions for the purpose of taking part in activities so specified'.

A supervision order may direct the responsible person to keep the supervisor informed of change of address, and to allow the supervisor to visit. The responsible person may be directed to ensure the child complies with the supervisor's programme, giving the order a better chance of success. The adult may be asked to attend a treatment centre, to benefit the family and enable the child to remain at home.

The county court has no jurisdiction to accept undertakings in care or supervision cases, *Re B (A Minor) (Supervision Order: Parental Undertaking)* [1996] 1 FLR 676.

The court has no jurisdiction to specify the activities in which the responsible person (with their consent) is to participate. This is for the supervisor to arrange. The supervisor can therefore direct a sex offender to have treatment *Re H (Minors) (Terms of Supervision Orders)* [1994] Fam Law 486.

The court may authorise medical or psychiatric examination, and also direct attendance by the child and/or carers for medical or psychiatric examination of the child, or, if necessary, in-patient or out-patient treatment, which a child of sufficient understanding has a right to refuse, see Chapter 13 below, and Sched 3 paras 4 and 5 Children Act. Although the supervisor has the power to direct attendance by the child for medical or psychiatric examination or assessment, only the court can authorise medical or psychological examination. Before making these directions, the court must know that satisfactory arrangements have been, or can be, made for the treatment proposed. This implies that the practitioners concerned have indicated that they agree to carry it out. If of sufficient understanding, the child's consent is also required. If a health practitioner is unwilling to continue treatment of the child, or the directions need altering because:

- the treatment should be extended beyond the period specified in the order;
- different treatment is required;
- the child is not susceptible to treatment; or
- no further treatment is required,

he must submit a written report to the supervisor, who will then have to put that report back to the court for revision of the directions, Sched 3 para 5(6)-(7) Children Act.

8.7.3 Enforcement

If there is a direction that the supervisor visits the child, and this is prevented, then the supervisor may bring the matter back to court for a warrant for a police officer to 'assist the supervisor to exercise these powers, using reasonable force if necessary', s 102(1) Children Act. Other conditions cannot specifically be enforced, but their breach can be justification for bringing the matter back before the court for an application to discharge the supervision order, to seek a care order, or for a different order to be made.

The Court of Appeal has held that if a local authority wants to substitute care for supervision, it needs a specific application for a care order and the s 31 threshold criteria must be proved in support of the care application, *Re A (Minor) (Supervision Extension)* [1995] 2 FCR 114 CA.

8.8 Removal of child from care

Local authorities have a duty to keep children subject to care orders while they are in force, s 33(1) Children Act. A parent, or anyone else, may not remove a child from the care of the local authority without leave of the court. Removal of a child without permission of the local authority or leave of the court, keeping a child away, or inciting a child to run away or stay away, is a criminal offence of child abduction under s 49 Children Act.

Note that if children are accommodated on a voluntary basis by a local authority, the situation is different in that they may be removed at any time by a person with parental responsibility for them. A local authority has no power to keep a child in voluntary accommodation where there is a person with parental responsibility ready and willing to look after the child, s 20 Children Act.

8.9 Variation, discharge and appeals

8.9.1 Variation and discharge

Applicant

Care orders cease when the child reaches 18, s 91(2) Children Act.

Supervision orders cease when directed by the court or on effluxion of time, see 8.7.1 above.

A care or supervision order may be varied or discharged on the application of:

- any person with parental responsibility for the child;
- the child (who does not need leave of the court);
- in the case of supervision, the supervisor;
- in the case of a care order, the local authority with the responsibility for the child.

The application needs to be on form C1. Leave, if required, is on form C2, with a draft application on C1 attached. The court should be that which made the original order. Other courts may accept the application if made with good reason.

Once made, the application may only be withdrawn with leave of the court, see r 5(1) FPC (CA) R 1991 and FPR 1991 r 4.5(1).

If the court discharges a care order it can order supervision, without having to re-prove the s 31(2) criteria, s 39(5) Children Act.

Following an unsuccessful application to discharge a care order, there is no further application without leave within six months, s 91(5) Children Act. Under s 91(14) the court can order no further applications without leave, but should use this power sparingly, see *Re G* [1996] 2 FCR 1.

Notice

Applications for discharge should be made on notice. The applicant should serve each person entitled to notice with form C6A, with the date and time of the hearing endorsed on it, at least seven days before first directions or hearing. See r 4(3) FPC (CA) R 1991 and FPR 1991 r 4.4(3). Those entitled to notice are the same as for the original application.

Respondents

Those who are entitled to be respondents should be served with a notice of the proceedings in form C6, together with a draft of the application on form C1, at least seven days before the first directions or hearing. See r 4(1)(b) FPC (CA) R 1991 and FPR 1991 r 4.4(1)(b).

Those entitled to be respondents are those who were entitled to be, or were, respondents in the original application.

8.9.2 Appeals

Appeals against decisions concerning care orders lie from the family proceedings court to the High Court, and from the county court and the High Court to the Court of Appeal, see Chapter 17 below.

On refusal to make a care order, or on discharge, the court has power to make a care order pending appeal, s 40(1) and (2) Children Act; or to declare that the order appealed shall not take effect pending appeal, s 40(3).

If the court of first instance refuses to make a care order pending appeal, the appeal court may make an interim care under s 38 Children Act.

9 Secure Accommodation

Secure accommodation is defined in s 25(1) Children Act 1989 (the 'Children Act') as 'accommodation provided for the purpose of restricting liberty'. Currently, the law relating to secure accommodation is complex, needing clarification. Children aged between 13 and 18 can be placed in secure accommodation for a variety of reasons. They may have committed a criminal offence and need to have their liberty restricted for their own safety or that of others. Orders made in these circumstances are called 'secure orders', to distinguish them from orders made in civil cases. A child who is looked after by a local authority, or in care to a local authority, may be kept in secure accommodation by the power given by a court order under s 25 Children Act. In certain circumstances, a child may be kept in secure accommodation by the consent of parents or those with parental responsibility.

Secure accommodation is currently governed by s 25 Children Act, by the Children (Secure Accommodation) Regulations 1991 SI 1991/1505 (the 'Secure Accommodation Regulations'); the Children (Secure Accommodation) (No 2) Regulations 1991 SI 1991/2034 and by the *Children Act 1989 Regulations and Guidance* Vol 4 *Residential Care* ('Residential Care'); Chapter 8 at pp 118–29. It is also mentioned in *Children Act Regulations and Guidance* Volume 1 *Court Orders* ('Court Orders') at para 5.1.

A child below the age of 13 years may not be kept in secure accommodation without authority of the Secretary of State, Reg 13(4), Secure Accommodation Regulations.

9.1 Effects of order

The effect of a secure accommodation order is restrict a child's liberty. Local authorities now have to pay careful regard to the guidance in their use of restriction of liberty. There is a distinction between placing a child in an environment (secure unit), from which he cannot run away and in which he is safeguarded; and the temporary restriction of a child's liberty, for example locking him in a room. There is a form of punishment colloquially called 'pindown', in which children who are disruptive or disobedient are punished by isolation in locked rooms and possibly with the additional deprivation of stimuli (removal of their radios, TVs, writing and reading materials, sometimes even clothes), for periods varying from hours to days. This type of punishment probably developed from a more moderate form of behavioural training called 'time out' to quieten overactive or disruptive children, which may still be used in working with children with learning difficulty, see *Helping Your Handicapped Child* by Janet Carr, Penguin, 1980, at p 93.

'Pindown' is a very severe form of 'time out', and has been much criticised in recent years because of the potentially emotionally abusive effect it can have on the child concerned. Some residential children's homes even had special rooms set aside for this purpose. *Residential Care* at para 8.10 emphasises that 'any practice or measure which prevents a child from leaving a room or building of his own free will may be deemed by the court to be a restriction of liberty.' In the community homes system, the liberty of children may only be restricted in secure accommodation approved by the Secretary of State. There are other secure units outside the community homes system, eg Youth Treatment Centres, which are covered by s 25.

Residential Care at para 8.14 is clear:

> ... subject to the exclusions mentioned in para 8.13 [Children detained under the Mental Health Act 1983] ... no child, other than one looked after by a local authority who is accommodated in the circumstances defined, may have his liberty restricted unless the statutory criteria for the use of secure accommodation in s 25(1) of the Children Act applies. This applies equally to any proposed short term placement of the child in a locked room for 'time out' or seclusion purposes. The maximum period such a child may be kept in secure accommodation without the authority of the court is 72 hours, whether consecutively or in aggregate in any period of 28 days.

So, we have to conclude that 'time out' as a behavioural approach to child care is still contemplated, but is now subject to stricter regulation.

Safeguards

- Restriction of liberty should constitute a last resort, para 5(1) of Court Orders.
- Secure placements should be only for so long as necessary.

- Regular inspection and review by:
  - Secretary of State (to approve secure unit);
  - Social Services Inspectorate (general running and facilities);
  - Department of Education (educational facilities);
  - Regional Placements Committee (placements);
  - Secure Accommodation Review Committee (resources).
- Time limits on the duration of secure accommodation orders.
- Care plans required by court on review of the orders.
- Each child has the right to an independent visitor.
- The 'three wise men (or women)'.

The local authority keeping a child in a secure unit must appoint at least three people, one of whom must not be a local authority employee, to review the placement within one month, and thereafter at three-monthly intervals. The task of these three is to ensure that the criteria justifying secure accommodation still applies, and that the placement is necessary, and no other description of accommodation is appropriate. See Reg 15, Secure Accommodation Regulations. The local authority must keep good case records, with details listed in Reg 17.

The safeguards in s 25 also cover children accommodated by the National Health Service Trusts and local education authorities.

9.1.1 Criminal cases

In criminal proceedings, a child may be remanded or bailed to local authority accommodation under s 23 Children and Young Persons Act 1969. Once there, the child may behave in such a way that there is concern that the child may abscond, or injure himself or others. If this concern is justified, then the local authority or other named persons (see application at 9.4 below) may seek a secure order. The complication in the law at the moment is that the routes to the order and the rules applicable vary according to the court to which the child has been remanded. The grounds for the application in each of these circumstances are set out in 9.3 below, and procedures at 9.4.

Juveniles may be detained by the police under circumstances specified in s 38 Police and Criminal Evidence Act 1984 ('PACE'), and under s 38(6), the juvenile shall be moved to local authority accommodation unless the custody officer certifies that either it is impracticable to do so, or in the case of a juvenile over 12 years old, no secure accommodation is available and other local authority accommodation would not be adequate to protect the public from serious harm from him. Remands of juveniles to local authority accommodation by the police in this way are covered by the provisions of s 25 Children Act. There are also safeguards for young people arrested, protecting their interests in detention and during questioning. For discussion of PACE and its implications in practice, see Michael Zander's book *Police and Criminal Evidence Act 1984*, Sweet & Maxwell, 3rd edn, 1995, London.

Under s 130 Criminal Justice Act 1988, if juvenile offenders are remanded to local authority accommodation, and placed in secure units, their time so spent will be deducted from their eventual custodial sentence. See also Local Authority Circular LAC (88) 23, which reminds local authorities to keep accurate records of the duration of detention of children in secure units for the sentencing court.

9.1.2 Use of secure accommodation in civil cases

Paragraph 8.6 *Residential Care* emphasises the local authority duty to 'take reasonable steps to avoid the need for children within their area to be placed in secure accommodation'. This duty is in Sched 2 para 7(c) Children Act, and also to 'encourage children within their area not to commit criminal offences', para 7(b). Placement decisions should be taken at a senior level, not lower than Assistant Director, accountable to the Director of Social Services. The placement should be part of the authority's overall plan for the child, and to safeguard and promote the child's welfare, s 22 Children Act.

9.2 Duration

Without the authority of the court, a child may only have his liberty restricted for up to 72 hours, either consecutively or in aggregate within any period of 28 consecutive days, Reg 10(1) Secure Accommodation Regulations. Reg 10(2) gives an exception where, if the court authorises secure accommodation for less than 28 days, on the day when the court order expires the 28 day period mentioned in Reg 10(1) starts running afresh from that day, ignoring any time spent in secure accommodation before the court order. Reg 10(3) gives special provisions for days either side of public holidays by granting a limited extension of the 72 hour time limit.

Where a child has been placed in local authority accommodation on a voluntary basis under s 20(1) Children Act, a person with parental responsibility can remove the child at any time, s 20(8), unless the exceptions in s 20(9) apply. This includes removal from secure accommodation.

9.2.1 Duration of court orders

Where the child has been remanded by a criminal court, the duration is for the period of the remand, with a maximum order of 28 days, Reg 13 Secure Accommodation Regulations.

If the child is committed to the Crown Court, then the period is up to three months on the first application, Reg 11, and up to six months on subsequent applications, Reg 12.

In the case of *In Re W (A Minor) (Secure Accommodation Order)* [1993] 1 FLR 692 it was held that the court should consider the shortest appropriate period, rather than order the maximum period available as a matter of course.

The maximum period is three months on first order, and any period in the secure unit before the order is made should be deducted from this. *C (Minor) v Humberside County Council and Another* [1995] 1 FCR 110. The justices making a care order had no power to order that a child kept in secure accommodation for a month should then be kept in the secure unit for a further three months.

The period of detention runs from the date the order was made, not the date the child was actually placed in the unit, see *Re B (Minor) (Secure Accommodation)* [1994] 2 FLR 707.

9.2.3 Adjournments

If there is an adjournment of an application for secure accommodation, then under s 25(5) Children Act , the court may permit the child to be kept secure during the adjournment. There is here an obvious risk of getting the order sought by the back door, perhaps without adequate proof of its necessity, particularly if the adjournment is for further evidence to become available. The court has provided a safeguard in stating that the adjournment may not be longer than the maximum periods for the order under Regs 11 and 12, see *C v Humberside County Council and Another* [1994] 2 FLR 759.

9.3 Grounds for application

Section 25 Children Act provides that if:
    (a) (i) the child has a history of absconding and is likely to abscond from any other description of accommodation; and

(ii) if he absconds he is likely to suffer significant harm; or

(b) that if he is kept in any other description of accommodation, he is likely to injure himself or others,

he can be placed in local authority accommodation by the court under s 23 Children and Young Persons Act 1969. This provision applies to children who are:

- charged with or convicted of an offence which would carry a sentence of 14 years or more for a person over 21 years old;
- charged with or convicted of an offence of violence, or who have a previous conviction for violence;
- detained under s 38(6) PACE.

The criteria for those placed under s 23 Children and Young Persons Act 1969 are differently worded from the criteria for those placed under Reg 6(2) Secure Accommodation Regulations. This regulation provides that a child may not be kept in secure accommodation unless it appears that any accommodation other than that provided for the purpose of restricting his liberty is inappropriate because:

- the child is likely to abscond from such accommodation;
- the child is likely to injure himself or other people if he is kept in any such accommodation.

Note that the likelihood of significant harm is omitted in this regulation. In the case of *Re M (A Minor) (Secure Accommodation Order)* [1995] 2 FCR 373 the welfare of the child was held by the court to be relevant, but not paramount in s 25 proceedings, and therefore application of the welfare checklist, although useful, was not obligatory. A child may be placed in a secure unit under s 25(1) to prevent her injuring another, which may be inconsistent with putting the welfare of the secured child first. The court's duty mirrors that of the local authority under s 20(1)(b) Children Act. The principles in s 1 are not designed to apply to Part III of the Children Act. The duty of the court is to ascertain whether the s 25 conditions are satisfied, and if they are then to make the order if this would be in accordance with the duty of the local authority to safeguard and promote the welfare of the child. The guardian ad litem will assist the court in deciding these questions. *Re M (Secure Accommodation Order)* [1995] Fam 108; [1995] 3 All ER 407, [1995]; 1 FLR 418 [1995]. Note that the Children Act Guidance and Regulations, Vols 1 and 4 mention the paramountcy of the welfare of the child in secure accommodation applications, and have now been overruled on this point by the court.

9.4 Practice and procedure

Secure accommodation orders are not included in the definition of family proceedings in s 8 Children Act, but because s 92(2) says that all proceedings under the Act are classed as family proceedings in the magistrates' court, this means that in the family proceedings court, s 25 applications are included. The 'menu' of orders available in family proceedings is open to the court, including s 8 orders and others which the court can make of its own volition, see Chapter 14 below.

9.4.1 Application

Where a child is being looked after by a local authority (even if the child is accommodated by another body) that local authority should be the applicant for the order. In other circumstances, other potential applicants include those who are providing accommodation for the child ie:

- local authority;
- health authority or NHS Trust;
- local education authority;
- person carrying on residential home, nursing home, or mental nursing home.

Once made, an application may only be withdrawn with leave of the court.

9.4.2 Forms

The application should be made on form C1 together with form C20 in accordance with Sched 1 Family Proceedings Courts (Children Act) Rules 1991, and App 1 Family Proceedings Rules 1991.

If the application is made to the High Court in wardship, it should be by summons, and the ward should be named as a party, r 5(5) Family Proceedings Rules 1991 as amended by the Family Proceedings (Amendment) Rules 1992 SI 1992/456.

9.4.3 Venue

Secure accommodation orders can be made at any level of the court. They can be made in criminal proceedings at the youth court or at a higher level of criminal court; and in the family proceedings courts, or the county court or High Court in the course of other proceedings.

9.4.4 Notice

Applications for secure accommodation must be made on one day's notice, r 4(4) Family Proceedings Courts (Children Act) Rules, and r 4.4(4) Family Proceedings Rules 1991.

The following people are entitled to notice of the proceedings, with the date, time and place of the hearing:
- local authority providing accommodation for the child;
- any person with whom the child was living at the time proceedings were commenced;
- person providing a refuge for the child.

Sch 2 Col (iv) Family Proceedings Courts (Children Act) Rules and App 3 Col (iii) Family Proceedings Rules 1991.

Rule 4(3) Family Proceedings Courts Children Act Rules, and r 4.4(3) Family Proceedings Rules 1991 provide that if a child is placed in a secure unit in a community home, and there is an application to keep the child there, certain people need to be informed as soon as practicable:
- the child's parents;
- any person with parental responsibility for the child;
- the child's independent visitor;
- any other person the local authority considers should be told.

9.4.5 Respondent

Certain people are automatically respondents to the application:
- those believed to have parental responsibility for the child;
- those who had parental responsibility prior to the care order, if one is in force;
- the child.

Others may be joined as respondents, and automatic respondents may be removed, r 7(1) Family Proceedings Courts Children Act Rules, and r 4.7(1) Family Proceedings Rules.

If the application is made to the High Court in wardship, the ward should be named as a party, r 5(5) Family Proceedings Rules as amended by the Family Proceedings (Amendment) Rules 1992 SI 1992/456.

9.4.6 Service

Service is effected on a solicitor for a party by delivery at his office, by first class post at the office or through the DX, or by fax to the office.

Service on a party who has no solicitor is by delivery to that party personally, or by delivery of first class post to his address. Rule 8 Family Proceedings Courts Children Act Rules, and r 4.8 Family Proceedings Rules.

Service on a child may be through her solicitor, or the guardian *ad litem*, or, with leave of the court, service on the child herself, r 8 (4) Family Proceedings Courts Children Act Rules, and r 4.8(4) Family Proceedings Rules.

The time for service may be abridged by the court, or waived altogether, see r 8(8) Family Proceedings Courts (Children Act) Rules, and r 4.8(8) Family Proceedings Rules.

9.5 Role of the guardian *ad litem*

These proceedings are 'specified proceedings' within the meaning of s 41 Children Act, and therefore a guardian *ad litem* must be appointed by the court unless it is of the opinion that it is unnecessary to do so in order to safeguard the child's interests. This is a protective measure intended to ensure that children in secure units have had their wishes and feelings made known to the court, and that the court has been advised of the most appropriate way forward in the best interests of the child. Children who are accommodated on a voluntary basis under s 20(1) Children Act are also safeguarded by this provision. See Chapter 16, para 16.1, for the role of the guardian *ad litem*.

9.6 Contact issues

Children in secure units have the right to reasonable contact with members of their family, as children in care. See Chapter 8 para 8.6.4. above. Since a s 25 application in a magistrates' court amounts to 'family proceedings' under s 8 Children Act, provided there is no care order in force, it is possible for the court to make a s 8 contact order to run alongside the secure accommodation order. A s 8 contact order can also co-exist with a supervision order. If the child is in care, then a s 34 care contact order may be made if necessary.

9.7 Rights of the child

These are:
- three persons to review placement, Reg 15, Children (Secure Accommodation) Regulations;
- duty on local authority to keep detailed case records, Reg 17;
- education whilst accommodated;
- entitlement to appropriate therapy where necessary;
- regular inspection of the secure unit by the Social Services Inspectorate from the Department of Health, who must approve the unit;
- inspection by the Department of Education, because children there are receiving education whilst accommodated;
- regional placement committees, who check the resources and conditions of the unit;
- time limits on the duration of secure accommodation orders;
- care plans on review of the orders;
- independent visitor;
- consultation, and to have wishes and feelings ascertained, s 22(4) Children Act;
- consultation with parents, and those with parental responsibility, s 22(4) Children Act;
- 'Free' legal aid to be represented on s 25 application.

9.7.1 Legal aid

Section 99 Children Act amends the Legal Aid Act 1988 ensuring legal aid is granted to a child subject to a s 25 Children Act application, who wishes to be legally represented. Legal aid is 'free', ie non-means and non-merits tested, available on completion of form CLA5A by the solicitor. The court may not make a secure accommodation order on an unrepresented child. The only exception is where the child has been informed of her right to apply for legal aid, and having been given the opportunity to do so, has failed to apply or refused to do so, s 25(6) Children Act.

9.8 Appeals

Section 94 Children Act makes provision for appeals to the High Court against decisions or refusals to authorise applications for the restriction of liberty. The placement in secure accommodation may continue whilst an appeal against authorisation is waiting to be determined. If the appeal is against a refusal to authorise the child may not be detained in a secure unit pending appeal. Appeals from the county court or High Court lie to the Court of Appeal, see Chapter 17 below.

10 Education Supervision Orders

Education between five and 16 years is compulsory. Section 39 Education Act 1944 authorises prosecution of parents who fail to ensure that their child receives a proper full time education suited to his age, ability and aptitude, and any special educational needs. An alternative to prosecution is an education supervision order.

Parents have the right under s 36 Education Act 1944 to educate their children other than in school, provided that they comply with s 39. The local education authority may help to arrange education otherwise than at school under s 56 Education Act 1944.

If parents fail to comply with s 39 Education Act 1944, they may be served with a notice requiring proof that the child is being properly educated. Failure to comply may result in a *school attendance order* requiring registration of the child at a named school, s 37 Education Act 1944. Failure to comply constitutes grounds for prosecution under s 37(5), or for a s 36 application.

10.1 Effects

Education supervision orders, under s 36 Children Act 1989 (the 'Children Act') place the child under the supervision of a local education authority. They differ from supervision orders made under s 31. School refusal may be evidence of neglect, lack of parental control, or underlying emotional problems, or the education system may be failing to meet the needs of the child. School refusal is no longer by itself a ground for care. It may form part of the s 31 grounds. See Chapter 8 above. In *Re O (A Minor) (Care Order: Education Procedure)* [1992] 2 FLR 7 Ewbank J supported a care order for a child who failed to attend school, holding that the child's intellectual, emotional and social development had been impaired such as to cause significant harm, sufficient to meet the s 31 criteria.

Paragraph 12, Sched 3 Children Act, states the supervisor's duty to 'advise assist and befriend' the child, to give directions to the parents and the child, and secure that he is properly educated, in consultation with child and parents, and to consider their wishes and feelings. Directions made should be reasonable, para 12, Sched 3. It is a defence to a prosecution to show that the directions were unreasonable, para 18(2)(b) Sched 3. Volume 7 *Guidance and Regulations* 'Guardians *ad litem* and other Court-Related Issues' discusses directions in paras 3.31-3.35. Directions might require the child to attend meetings with the supervisor or with teachers at the school to discuss progress, or cover medical assessment or examination, or assessment by a clinical psychologist. They should be confirmed in writing, and the parents informed. Persistent failure to comply with directions without good cause may lead to prosecution.

Under Sched 3 para 13 Children Act, parents lose their right to have the child educated at home, or move the child to another school, while an education supervision order is in force, and they have no right of appeal against admissions decisions.

The *Guidance* Vol 7 is made under s 7 Local Authority Social Services Act 1970, and so local authorities must follow it unless there are cogent local reasons not to comply. Non-compliance with Chapter 3 is *prima facie* ground for complaint, and will have to be justified if challenged. However, in *Essex County Council v B* [1993] 1 FLR 866 the court held that the local education authority is not bound by the *Guidance*.

10.2 Duration

The order will subsist for one year, or until the child is no longer of compulsory school age, whichever is the earlier, para 15, Sched 3, Children Act. It may be discharged earlier, on the application of the child, the parents, or the local education authority, para 17(1) Sched 3 Children Act.

It may be extended for up to three years if application is made within three months before the expiry date, and it can be extended more than once, para 15 Sched 3.

10.3 Grounds for application

Under s 36(3), an order may only be made if the court is 'satisfied that the child concerned is of compulsory school age and is not being properly educated.'

'Proper education' is defined in s 36(4) as 'receiving efficient full-time education suitable for his age, ability and aptitude, and special educational needs he may have.'

Where a child is the subject of a 'school attendance order' under s 37 Education Act 1944 which is in force but with which the child is not complying, or is a registered pupil of a school which he is not attending regularly, there is a presumption that the child is not being properly educated, s 36(5).

Note that an order may not be sought in respect of a child who is already subject to a care order, s 36(6).

Section 36(8) requires education to consult social services. Volume 7 para 3(18) requires everyone to make all reasonable efforts to resolve a problem of poor school attendance without the use of legal sanctions: 'Many attendance difficulties can be overcome by sensitive action by schools and the Education Welfare Service.' Paragraph 3.10 requires the outcome of the consultation to be confirmed in writing, indicating whether the social services department is involved with the child or the family, and if there are any known reasons why an education supervision order would not be appropriate. The social services department may seek the assistance of the education authority in the provision of services for the child, who are under a duty to comply with the request in accordance with s 27(1)-(3) Children Act. There is a reciprocal arrangement in s 27(4) which also requires every local authority to assist any local education authority with the provision of services for any child within the local authority's area who has special educational needs.

10.4 Practice and procedure

10.4.1 Application

The applicant is the local education authority. The application should be made on form C17. Applications are 'family proceedings' under s 8(3) and (4) Children Act, see Chapter 14. The principles in s 1 Children Act apply, see Chapter 3.

10.4.2 Venue

Cases should be commenced in the family proceedings court, but may be transferred to the county court or the High Court. If the county court or the High Court has directed an investigation of the child's circumstances under s 37(1) Children Act, the application may be made to that court or a nominated care centre. If there are proceedings pending in a court, then the application may commence there.

10.4.3 Notice

Rule 9(3)(4) Family Proceedings Court (Children Act 1989) Rules 1991 SI 1991/1395, and r 4.9(3)(4) Family Proceedings Rules 1991 SI 1991/1247, provide that seven days' notice of the hearing or directions appointment must be given. Notice is of the date and venue of the application.

A local authority, or the manager of a refuge providing accommodation for the child may be served with notice of the application, r 4 Family Proceedings Court (Children Act) Rules and r 4.4 Family Proceedings Rules.

10.4.4 Respondents

Every person with parental responsibility for the child is a respondent, as is the child. Respondents should be served with notice of the application and a copy of the application itself. Respondents may file and serve an answer two days before the hearing.

10.4.5 Service

The normal rules of service apply, see r 4 Family Proceedings Court (Children Act) Rules and r 4.4 Family Proceedings Rules. The court also has power under the rules to vary or waive service.

10.5 Rights of the child

These are:
- the child's welfare is paramount;
- to be consulted on schooling issues;
- to have wishes and feelings taken into consideration;
- to be a respondent in the application if of sufficient age and understanding;
- to receive directions that are reasonable;
- to advice, assistance and befriending from the supervisor.

10.6 Variation, discharge and appeals

The maximum duration of a first order is one year, a lesser period ordered by the court, or expiry when the child exceeds compulsory school age.

Discharge can be on the application of the child, the parents, or the local education authority, para 17(1) Sched 3 Children Act. The court on discharge may order the local authority to investigate the child's circumstances under s 37 and para 17(2) Sched 3 Children Act.

The order may be extended for up to three years on application by the authority within three months before the expiry date, and the order can be extended more than once, para 15 Sched 3 Children Act.

Appeals

Appeal from the magistrates lies to the High Court, s 49 Children Act. Orders made in the county court or High Court may be appealed to the Court of Appeal, see Chapter 17 below.

11 Police Powers under the Children Act 1989

Police have special powers under s 46 Children Act 1989 referred to as 'police protection', which do not need a court order. The ground for action is that police have reasonable cause to believe the child would otherwise suffer significant harm, s 46(2).

These powers are:

- to remove a child to a safe place and keep him there, s 46(1)(a);
- to prevent a child's removal from a safe place, s 46(1)(b);
- no power to enter premises without a warrant unless s 17 Police and Criminal Evidence Act 1984 satisfied (s 17 includes saving life and limb, prevention of serious damage to property, or arrests);
- police must safeguard and promote the child's welfare, s 46(9)(b).

The maximum duration for the exercise of s 46 powers is 72 hours, s 46(6).

Each area must have a 'designated police officer', responsible for carrying out the duties imposed by the Children Act, who can apply for emergency protection if necessary, ss 46(3)(e), and 46(7).

The police must, under s 46(3), inform the local authority of their action, the reasons for it, and the child's whereabouts; inform the child and discover her wishes and feelings; remove the child to local authority accommodation, and, under s 46(4), take reasonable steps to inform parents, those with parental responsibility, and those with whom the child was living, of the action, the reasons for it, and future plans.

12 Case Preparation and Advocacy in Child Law

12.1 Preparation of the case

Good advocacy is not an ability to speak persuasively in court. It is good preparation. Good advocates are clear, concise and accurate, and they read the papers thoroughly before the hearing. Basic knowledge of evidence, relevant case law and procedural rules is essential; see the book list in Chapter 19.

12.2 Burden of proof in child law cases

Generally, the person alleging a fact must prove it. In child protection, it is a balance of probability, ie 'it is more likely than not' that there is actual or a potential risk of significant harm to the child. In *Re H and Others (Minors) (Sexual Abuse: Standard of Proof)* [1996] 1 FLR 80, and 1 FCR 509 the House of Lords considered the standard of proof of sexual abuse, concluding 'the more serious the allegation, the less likely it is that the event occurred, and, hence, the stronger should be the evidence before the court concludes that the allegation is established on a balance of probability' *per* Lord Nicholls of Birkenhead.

12.3 Special evidence rules in child law cases

Child law cases should be non-adversarial. The focus of the case is the welfare of the child. Evidence law in child protection is different from other areas of law. The Children Act makes special rules encouraging admission of actions affecting the child without these becoming the basis for prosecution. In wardship proceedings the strict rules of evidence do not apply, see Butler-Sloss LJ in *Re H (Minor), Re K (Minors) (Child abuse: Evidence)* [1989] 2 FLR 313 at pp 332-33. The general rules of evidence in non-child law cases render certain evidence inadmissible, ie character, hearsay, evidence obtained by illicit means (eg covert video surveillance) and opinion.

12.3.1 Character

In child law cases, consideration of the character of those who care for the child is vitally important, and evidence which tends to show their characteristics is admitted.

12.3.2 Best evidence and hearsay

If notes are produced, the court requires the original notes made contemporaneously, not neatly typed copies made later on. Notes should be written up at the time or as soon as possible after the event recorded. If notes are made days later their reliability may be questioned.

Witnesses are required only to give an account of what they themselves actually experienced as evidence of the truth. If a witness tells the court what someone else said, the words quoted cannot be admitted as proof that the things said really happened. If A tells the court that on 14 July B said to him, 'C hit me', this is admissible to prove that on that day B was alive and able to speak, and that he spoke to A and A heard his words, but it is not sufficient to prove that C did in fact hit B. B would have to give evidence of this personally.

In child law cases, however, the court requires all relevant evidence. The wishes and feelings of children are important, and quotations from others about the child or of what the child said can be vital. Section 96(3) Children Act, and the Children (Admissibility of Hearsay Evidence) Order 1993, SI 1993/621, provide that in civil proceedings before the High Court or a county court, and family proceedings, and civil proceedings in a magistrates' court under the Child Support Act 1991, evidence given in connection with the upbringing, maintenance or welfare of a child, shall be admissible notwithstanding any rule of law relating to hearsay. Family proceedings are defined in s 8(3) and s 105 Children Act. Refer to s 6(3) Civil Evidence Act 1968 for helpful criteria in assessment of hearsay evidence.

12.3.3 Opinion

Witnesses give factual or expert evidence. Witnesses of fact may not give their opinion and are expected to restrict themselves to a full and accurate account of what happened. The court draws inferences from the facts. Experts may draw inferences, and offer opinions based on the facts, research and their own learning and experience. They should behave in a professional manner, and be impartial.

12.3.4 Documents cited by guardian *ad litem*

Under s 41(11)(a)-(b) Children Act, the court may take account of any statement contained in the report of a guardian *ad litem*, and of any evidence given in respect of matters referred to in the guardian's report. The guardian *ad litem* has access to, and may cite, local authority records, s 42(2) Children Act. The court has the power to regulate its own proceedings, and will assess the weight to give to such evidence.

12.3.5 No professional privilege for medical reports

There are recent cases concerning disclosure of expert evidence obtained by a party which does not assist his case. Thorpe J in *Essex County Council v R (A Minor)* [1993] 2 FLR 826 held that where the welfare of the child is paramount, there should be a duty to disclose medical evidence, even if it is unfavourable, in the interests of the child.

In *Oxfordshire County Council v M* [1994] 1 FLR 175 the Court of Appeal upheld this principle. Lord Justice Steyn referred in his judgment to 'expert reports', and it is submitted that if this is correctly reported, then the principle may be interpreted more widely than in the case of medical reports, and logically should cover all expert reports in Children Act proceedings. Communications between lawyer and client remain privileged.

12.4 Directions hearings – ordering the evidence

Most of us use expert witnesses on a fairly regular basis, developing good working relationships. See Chapter 18 below for instruction of experts, judicial guidance, how to find the right expert and resource issues. Before the directions hearing the advocate should ascertain whether experts can undertake the work, how long it will take, cost, legal aid and any assistance required. The advocate also needs to take instructions about the venue of any tests to be carried out, who should accompany the parties/child and what should be done with the results of the expert's inquiry. Dates to avoid must be known, enabling the court to fix a suitable hearing date. Delay must be avoided, s 1(3) Children Act. Leave is required for disclosure of documents to experts, and for medial or psychiatric examinations or assessments of children.

12.5 Court procedure at the hearing

Procedure is addressed separately in the chapters dealing with each order. However, hearings follow a reasonably consistent pattern common to most Children Act applications.

12.5.1 Notes of Evidence

There is a duty on the court to take a note of the 'substance of oral evidence given' at the proceedings, r 20 Family Proceedings (Children Act 1989) Rules 1991 and r 4.20 Family Proceedings Rules 1991.

12.5.2 Order of Evidence

Rule 21(2) Family Proceedings (Children Act 1989) Rules 1991 and r 4.21(2) Family Proceedings Rules 1991 empower the court to regulate its own proceedings, eg vary the order of speeches and evidence to suit the needs of the case and the people involved.

Unless the courts do create a variation of procedure, r 21(3) and r 4.21(3) respectively set out the order of evidence:

- applicant;
- any party with parental responsibility for the child;
- other respondents (including a child who is separately represented);
- the guardian *ad litem*;
- the child, if he is not a party and there is no guardian *ad litem* (this is an unusual situation which would apply in private law cases, since in most Part IV cases there is a guardian *ad litem* appointed, and a child of sufficient age to instruct a lawyer separately will be a party).

12.5.3 Extent of evidence

There are some limitations on the courts regulating their own proceedings. They must hear some evidence, even if the matter is agreed. It is not normally sufficient to file statements and to rely on these to support a case, calling no oral evidence at all, although this may occur in exceptional circumstances. In *Re B (Minors) (Contact)* [1994] 2 FLR 1 Butler-Sloss LJ in the Court of Appeal, hearing an issue of defined contact, gave guidance to the courts on approaching the matter of how much evidence is appropriate, at p 6A(1)-(6).

In *Re F (Minor) (Care Order: Procedure)* [1994] 1 FLR 240 a magistrates' court which had heard evidence from the local authority but refused to hear the evidence of the father was held to be quite wrong. The justices should have heard the evidence from both sides or none at all.

Figure 14: Admissible evidence in care proceedings

ORAL EVIDENCE may be given by:		ANY WITNESS MAY PRODUCE ALL OR ANY OF THESE:	
		Photographs	Provided produced by taker, who has unretouched negatives and can produce originals
The child themselves ...	Provided that the court is satisfied on enquiry that they understand the duty to tell the truth	Tape recordings	Provided shown to be original and not tampered with
Any witness of fact	Hearsay rule not applicable in family proceedings. Witness may not give opinions.	X rays	As photographs
		Other objects	eg clothing, weapons, admissible provided relevant
An expert witness	May give fact and opinion, can refer to charts, notes, tables and reference works	Video recordings	If of an incident, admissible as photograph. Admissibility and content of interviews may be questioned

Notes may be used provided that They were made contemporaneously with events, or sufficiently soon thereafter for the memory of the person making the note to be clear.

DOCUMENTARY EVIDENCE:
May be admissible provided it complies with s1 Evidence Act 1938. Personal knowledge of facts/or statement of fact is or forms part of continuous record in which the maker recorded facts given by another who had personal knowledge of them and maker gives evidence. Medical notes come into this category. Special rules for computer records. Copies may be accepted for same reason if certified to be true copies. Documents copied by the GAL may be adduced in evidence, s 42 CA 1989.

SELF-PRODUCING DOCUMENTS:
memorandum of conviction	Admissible under s 11 Civil Evidence Act 1968 and r 68 Magistrates Court Rules 1981
school attendance records	Admissible under s 95 Education Act 1944
medical certificate	Admissible under s 26 CYPA 1963.

Figure 15: Directions hearing checklist

- **LIST OF WITNESSES**
  - client
  - other parties
- **DATES TO AVOID**
  - parties
  - witnesses of fact
  - expert witnesses
  - own dates to avoid
- **INFORMATION/ASSISTANCE REQUIRED BY WITNESSES OR CLIENT**
  - reference material
  - exhibits
  - interpreter
  - visual aids in court/TV links/tape recorder or player
  - security
  - wheelchair access, hearing loop, etc
- **INFORMATION AVAILABLE FOR EXPERTS**
  - documents in case, and/or list
    (leave required for disclosure to expert)
  - exhibits to be sent to expert or in expert's possession
  - chronology
  - conference of experts required
- **LEAVE OF THE COURT/OR CONSENTS REQUIRED**
  - disclosure of documents, information, exhibits
  - medical or psychiatric examinations and their venue, who will accompany child, to whom results are to be given
  - special testing (does it need High Court, eg HIV?)
  - excuse party/child attendance at court
  - accommodation of child

- **STATEMENTS/REPORTS TO FILE?**
  - parties
  - witnesses
  - experts
  - chronology
  - reports
  - other documents from files
- **STATEMENTS/REPORTS NOT FILED OR LATE?**
  - consent required
- **SERVICE**
  - applicant and parties
  - those entitled to notice of the proceedings
  - those entitled to be respondents
  - guardian *ad litem*

12.5 Courtroom skills

12.5.1 Court manners

Proceedings are non-adversarial, and in an inevitably emotional situation, a calm advocate can assist everyone greatly.

Dress should be unobtrusive. Leave coats, bags, umbrellas etc in the advocate's room, if there is one. Bring into court only those things which are necessary.

Titles	
Magistrates	Your Worship, Sir or Madam
Deputy/District Judge	Sir or Madam
County Court Judge	Your Honour
High Court and Court of Appeal Judge	My Lord or My Lady (usually pronounced by the Bar as M'Lord or M'Lady)
Barristers and solicitors referring to each other	My friend, Counsel for X ..., or Mrs ... or Mr ...

The applicant's advocate introduces other advocates and parties to the court. Find out their names before going in. Greet other parties and advocates on arrival at court, letting the court usher know of your arrival. Ushers enter the names of everyone present on their court list. Stand while the judge or bench enters the room, and allow them to sit before sitting yourself. Figure 16 (p 100) illustrates a typical Family Proceedings courtroom layout and seating.

The family proceedings courts and county courts may conduct their proceedings seated. Check with the clerk to the court. The general rule for advocates or witnesses is to stand until invited to sit, or, if feeling unwell or infirm, to ask leave to be seated.

Don't interrupt another advocate when addressing the court. Allow them to finish, then request the court's permission to correct factual or legal errors. Making audible critical 'asides' to other advocates or clients is not acceptable, and is unprofessional.

Bring to court sufficient copies of documents and draft orders for all the parties who need to have one. The original goes to the judge or bench, with a copy to the clerk.

Put the case papers in a ring binder with strong clips that won't come open unexpectedly. Mark up the pages to which reference is to be made, and number them to accord with bundles filed with the court. Make it easy to find relevant materials quickly.

The examination of witnesses follows the order of evidence (see above). Each witness is called to the witness box by the party calling him, sworn in or requested to affirm and examined in chief. Questions which suggest an answer are 'leading questions' and forbidden in examination in chief; this is 'leading the witness'. Ask 'What time of day was it?' not 'Was it three o'clock?' The other parties may then cross-examine the witness. Finally, the party calling the witness may re-examine to clarify points already made. The court should then be offered the opportunity to ask questions of the witness. Ask permission for the witness to leave the court, if not required further.

Traditionally, the applicant opens the case and outlines their case to the court. The other parties then have the opportunity to make a speech to the court but usually do so at the end of the case. The guardian *ad litem* or their advocate will be the last to speak. If there are submissions on law during the case, the order of address follows the order of evidence.

When the case is completed, stand to allow the judge to leave the room.

Figure 16: Layout of typical Family Proceedings Court

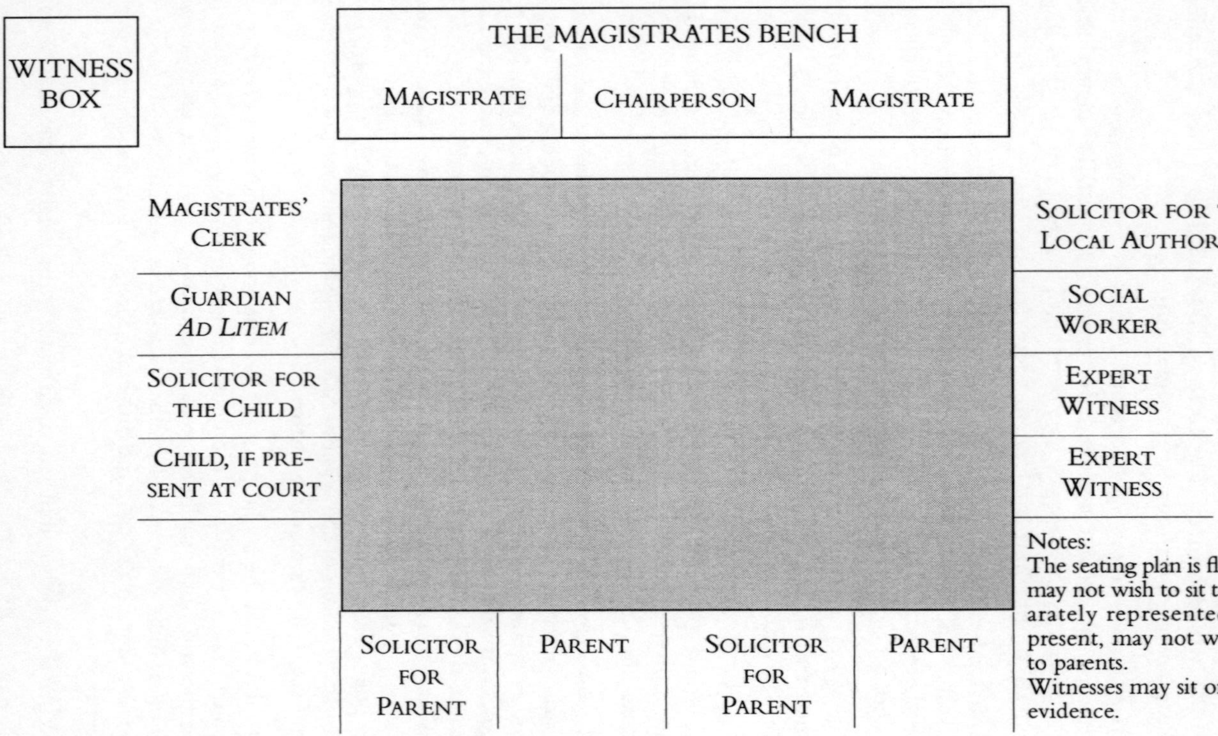

```
┌─────────────┐      ┌──────────────────────────────────────────┐
│   WITNESS   │      │         THE MAGISTRATES BENCH            │
│     BOX     │      │  MAGISTRATE │ CHAIRPERSON │ MAGISTRATE   │
└─────────────┘      └──────────────────────────────────────────┘
```

Positions around the court:

- Magistrates' Clerk
- Guardian Ad Litem
- Solicitor for the Child
- Child, if present at court
- Solicitor for the Local Authority
- Social Worker
- Expert Witness
- Expert Witness
- Parent
- Solicitor for Parent
- Parent
- Solicitor for Parent

Notes:
The seating plan is flexible. Parents may not wish to sit together if separately represented. A child, if present, may not wish to sit next to parents.
Witnesses may sit or stand to give evidence.

13 Children's Rights

13.1 To accept or refuse medical treatment

No adult or child competent to make their own medical decisions may be given medical treatment without their consent. Breach may incur liability for damages for assault, or constitute an offence in criminal law. Detention in hospital or any other place without consent could constitute false imprisonment.

At what age can a child give her own consent?

13.1.1 Children over 16

Under s 8 Family Law Reform Act 1969, at the age of 16, a young person gains the right to give informed consent to surgical, medical or dental treatment. Examinations or assessments must impliedly be included. A young person with mental illness, disability, or psychiatric disturbance is subject to the Mental Health Acts. A person with parental responsibility (see Chapter 4) for a child under 18 may give consent to treatment, an examination or assessment of the child. Such a person's consent has equal validity to that of the child.

13.1.2 Children under 16

In *Gillick v West Norfolk and Wisbech Area Health Authority* [1986] AC 112 the House of Lords formulated the concept now known colloquially as '*Gillick* competence' in which the ability of a child under 16 to make her own medical decisions is evaluated according to chronological age considered in conjunction with the child's mental and emotional maturity, intelligence and comprehension. Lord Scarman said: 'It will be a question of fact whether a child seeking advice has sufficient understanding of what is involved to give a consent valid in law. Until the child achieves the capacity to consent, the parental right to make the decision continues save only in exceptional circumstances.

Emergency, parental neglect, abandonment of the child, or inability to find the parent are examples of exceptional situations ...'

Gillick competence has been reviewed in a number of subsequent cases. In *Re S (Minor) (Refusal of Treatment)* [1995] 1 FCR 604 it was held that a girl of almost 16 suffering from thalassaemia major should continue with her treatment, despite her refusal to do so on religious grounds. The discontinuance of treatment would have resulted in her death within a few weeks. The court acknowledged that at 18 she could refuse, and effectively end her life, but expressed the hope that in the intervening period she might change her mind, or that gene therapy would relieve her condition.

Understanding potential consequences of refusing treatment or assessment increases with age and maturity, influenced by the information provided, the child's intelligence and level of understanding. The National Health Service *Guide to Consent for Examination or Treatment* recommends doctors should record factual information given to the child, including questions asked and the child's responses, for possible reference later if the child's ability to make the decision were to be questioned. Where a child is seen alone, efforts should be made to obtain agreement to inform parents save where this is clearly not in the child's best interests.

13.1.3 Mentally disordered children

Where a child is mentally ill or mentally disordered, and unable to make a legally valid decision for himself, the High Court in its wardship jurisdiction may consent on behalf of a person under 18. The safeguards in the Mental Health Act 1983 apply. Section 131(2) allows parents to arrange for the informal admission of children under 16 to hospital for treatment for mental disorder, the admission of those over 16 if they are incapable of making their own decisions or expressing their own wishes. The definition of 'nearest relative' in s 27(2) Mental Health Act 1983 is now amended to substitute for the word 'mother' mother and father with parental responsibility.

13.1.4 Where nobody has parental responsibility

In situations where an immediate decision or action is needed and no one with parental responsibility is available, s 3(5) Children Act provides:

A person who:

(a) does not have parental responsibility for a particular child; but

(b) has care of the child,

may ... do what is reasonable in all the circumstances of the case for the purpose of safeguarding or promoting the child's welfare.

13.2 To accept or refuse medical or psychiatric assessment

Child protection often necessitates medical or psychiatric examination or assessment. The report of the inquiry into child abuse in Cleveland of 1997 demonstrated that repeated medical examinations can themselves be abusive. The court has wide power to set limits by directions, eg the place and time of an examination; person(s) to be present; person(s) to conduct the examination; and person(s) or authorities to whom the results shall be given.

13.2.1 Circumstances in which the court may direct medical or psychiatric examination or assessment, which the child has a right to refuse:

- interim care order;
- interim supervision order;
- emergency protection order;
- child assessment order.

In supervision orders, the child may be directed to undergo a medical, but not a psychiatric examination, and the court may only make this a condition of the order if the child consents.

Where the child has the right to refuse medical or psychiatric examinations, his wishes and feelings must be ascertained by the guardian ad litem, or doctor, see paras 3.50-3.51 Guidance and Regulations, Vol 1 'Court Orders'. Doctors must check whether the child is capable of giving an informed decision, and that he consents, before proceeding. If, when the child is with the doctor she refuses, then the doctor should not proceed, and should refer the matter back to the court. If the court agrees that this is an informed decision, then usually it will respect it, but if the refusal may place the child in serious danger, then the High Court may overrule the refusal in the child's best interests.

13.3 To make his or her own application to the court

Under s 10(8) Children Act children of sufficient age and understanding may make their own applications for s 8 orders, with leave.

Following *Re SC (Minor) (Leave to Seek Residence Order)* [1994] 1 FLR 96 where the child is the applicant, then his welfare is paramount, because the provisions of s 10(9) do not apply. Also, everyone with parental responsibility for the child should have notice of the application. Section 10(9) sets out the criteria for the court's consideration in granting leave for all other applicants, and it has been held that the child's welfare is not paramount in these applications, see Chapter 14, para 14.2.2 below. Note: all applications by a child for leave to seek a s 8 order should be heard in the High Court – *Practice Direction* [1993] 1 All ER 820; [1993] 1 FLR 668.

Children may seek other orders under the Children Act, with leave, including discharge of:

- care;
- supervision;
- emergency protection;
- s 8 orders;
- parental responsibility orders;
- parental responsibility agreements.

The decision as to whether a child is of sufficient age and understanding to apply is a matter initially for the solicitor instructed by the child, but ultimately for the court to decide *Re CT (Minor) (Wardship: Representation)* [1993] 3 WLR 602; [1993] 2 FLR 278. The court could appoint a next friend for the child, usually the Official Solicitor, under r 9.2A(10)(b) and r 9(5) Family Proceedings Rules 1991.

13.4 To disagree with the guardian *ad litem* and instruct a solicitor separately

Where children are subject to care or supervision applications, their solicitors are appointed by their guardians *ad litem* or the court. A child of sufficient age and understanding may disagree with the guardian *ad litem*, remaining a party with his own solicitor. The guardian will notify the court and continue unrepresented, or appoint another solicitor. Procedure is governed by rr 11(3), 12(1)(a), and 12(3)-(5) Family Proceedings (Children Act) Rules; and rr 4.11(3), 4.12(1)(a), and 4.12(3)-

(5) Family Proceedings Rules 1991. The duties and responsibilities of the solicitor for the child are set out in the Law Society Guidance and the Solicitors Family Law Association Guidance, see Chapter 16 below at 16.1.

13.5 Rights of a child in care

A child in care has rights protected by the Children Act and also by the *Guidance* issued under it. The child has a right to:

- refuse medical or psychiatric assessment ordered within an interim care order under s 38(6) Children Act;
- refuse medical or psychiatric assessment in specified circumstances, see above at 13.2;
- reasonable contact with his family, see 'contact' in Chapter 8, at 8.6.4. above, and paras 9 and 13-16 'Principles and Practice' in *Guidance;*
- be consulted on issues involving her care, see paras 2.21 and 6.4, Guidance and Regulations Vol 3; also paras 2.21, 2.45, *Guidance and Regulations,* Vol 4, ss 22(4), 61 and 64 Children Act, and para 25 'Principles and Practice' in *Guidance* Vol 4;
- have his race, culture, religion and background taken into account in care proceedings, s 1 Children Act and para 4, 'Principles and Practice' in *Guidance;*
- consult a solicitor of her own if of sufficient age and understanding, see above at 13.4;
- develop a sense of identity, para 19, 'Principles and Practice' in *Guidance;*
- grow to independence, para 26 'Principles and Practice' in *Guidance.*
- to live in peace and safety, free from abuse, para 3, 'Principles and Practice' in *Guidance;*
- regular reviews of his care plan, and involvement in the planning in a way appropriate to his age and understanding, paras 3.8, 3.11(a), 3.15, *Guidance and Regulations* Vol 4;
- the child's wishes should also be taken into account when planning for placements, and for future care; para 3.20; also ss 22(4), 61 and 64 Children Act, and para 25, 'Principles and Practice' in *Guidance.*

14 Other Children Act Orders available to the Court

The Children Act 1989 ('Children Act') empowers the court to make orders of its own volition in 'family proceedings', defined in s 8(3). The court cannot intervene to impose orders for care, supervision, secure accommodation, emergency protection or child assessment. There is a 'menu' of orders available in family proceedings, from which the court may choose, subject to the principles of s 1 Children Act, and in particular, that the court should make no order unless it is necessary for the welfare of the child, see Chapter 3.

14.1 Orders in family proceedings

Orders available in family proceedings are shown in Fig 17 (p 109) Family Assistance Orders require no application, but the parties must agree to their making.

14.2 Section 8 orders

Section 8(1) Children Act creates the s 8 orders: contact, prohibited steps, residence and specific issue, available in all family proceedings. The court may regulate, on an application or of its own volition, the child's residence and contact with others; prohibit specified steps without leave of the court; and deal with any specific issues arising in the child's upbringing.

OTHER CHILDREN ACT ORDERS AVAILABLE TO THE COURT 107

Figure 17 Family proceedings under the Children Act 1989

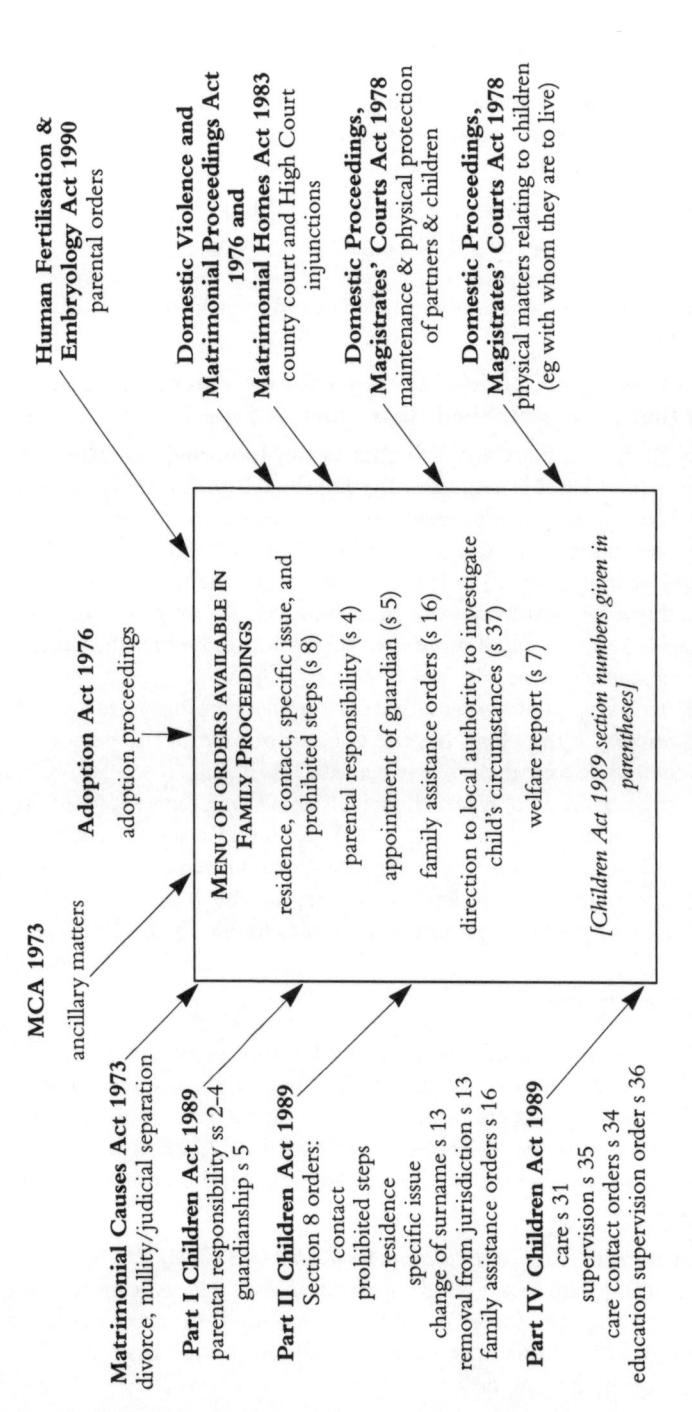

MCA 1973
ancillary matters

Human Fertilisation & Embryology Act 1990
parental orders

Adoption Act 1976
adoption proceedings

Domestic Violence and Matrimonial Proceedings Act 1976 and Matrimonial Homes Act 1983
county court and High Court injunctions

Domestic Proceedings, Magistrates' Courts Act 1978
maintenance & physical protection of partners & children

Domestic Proceedings, Magistrates' Courts Act 1978
physical matters relating to children (eg with whom they are to live)

Matrimonial Causes Act 1973
divorce, nullity/judicial separation

Part I Children Act 1989
parental responsibility ss 2–4
guardianship s 5

Part II Children Act 1989
Section 8 orders:
  contact
  prohibited steps
  residence
  specific issue
  change of surname s 13
  removal from jurisdiction s 13
  family assistance orders s 16

Part IV Children Act 1989
care s 31
supervision s 35
care contact orders s 34
education supervision order s 36

MENU OF ORDERS AVAILABLE IN FAMILY PROCEEDINGS

residence, contact, specific issue, and prohibited steps (s 8)

parental responsibility (s 4)

appointment of guardian (s 5)

family assistance orders (s 16)

direction to local authority to investigate child's circumstances (s 37)

welfare report (s 7)

[Children Act 1989 section numbers given in parentheses]

Applications listed outside the central box are 'family proceedings' as defined by the Children Act 1989, s 105 and s 8(3). Each of the orders in the central box may be made by the court in family proceedings.

14.2.1 Who can apply as of right?

Some applicants are entitled to apply, and others must first seek the leave of the court. The following are entitled under s 10 Children Act to apply for any s 8 order:

(a) any parent or guardian of a child, s 10(4)(a) (this will include the unmarried father of a child whether or not he has parental responsibility);
(b) any person in whose favour a residence order is in force with respect to the child, s 10(4)(b).

The following are entitled to apply for a residence or contact order (but not a prohibited steps order or a specific issue order):

(a) any party to a marriage (whether or not subsisting) in relation to whom the child is a child of the family, s 10(5)(a) (this provision enables a step-parent to seek a residence or contact order);
(b) any person with whom the child has lived for a period of at least three years, s 10(5)(b) (s 10(10) provides that the three year period need not be continuous but must have begun not more than five years before, or ended more than three months before, the making of the application);
(c) (i) any person who, where there is a residence order in force with respect to the child, has the consent of each of the persons in whose favour the order is made, s 10(5)(c)(i);
 (ii) any person who, where there is a care order in force, has the consent of the local authority, s 10(5)(c)(ii) (but note, the court can only make a residence order in such circumstances);
 (iii) any person who, in any other case, has the consent of each of those (if any) with parental responsibility for the child, s 10(5)(c)(iii).

14.2.2 Leave to apply

Any other person needs leave to apply for a s 8 order, including the child. The court must be satisfied a child has sufficient understanding to make the proposed application, and the application must be made to the High Court, see *Practice Direction* [1993] 1 All ER 820. The Court of Appeal has said that this is a 'serious step' which should not be taken lightly.

Note that in *Re A (Care: Discharge Application by a Child)* [1995] 1 FLR 599 Thorpe J held that a child's application to discharge care was not one which required leave of the court. An application by a child in statutory care for a residence order, if successful, would have the effect of discharging the care order.

14.2.3 Considerations on application for leave

Section 10(9) requires that on applications for leave the court should have regard to various considerations which do not include the paramountcy principle. On the issue of leave, the welfare of the child is not of paramount importance because an application for leave is not a trial of the substantive issue, see *North Yorkshire County Council v G* [1993] 2 FLR 732. If, however, the child is the applicant, then s 10(9) does not apply, see *Re C (Minor) (Leave to seek s 8 order)* [1994] 1 FLR 96.

Section 10(9) sets out the matters to be taken into account:

(a) the nature of the proposed application;
(b) the applicant's connection with the child;
(c) any risk that there might be of that proposed application disrupting the child's life to such an extent that he would be harmed by it; and
(d) where the child is being looked after by a local authority:
  (i) the authority's plans for the child's future; and
  (ii) the wishes and feelings of the child's parents.

14.2.4 Duration

Section 8 orders subsist until the child reaches 16, unless they are brought to an end earlier by the court, or made of limited duration, s 91(11) Children Act. They may in exceptional circumstances be extended until the child reaches 18 years of age, s 9(6) Children Act.

It has been held recently that there is no such animal as an 'interim residence order' but instead, only a residence order of limited duration.

14.2.5 When the court may not make a s 8 order

- Section 9(1) Children Act establishes restrictions on making s 8 orders:

  No court shall make any s 8 order, other than a residence order, with respect to a child who is in the care of a local authority.

A residence order will result in the automatic discharge of the care order, s 91(1) Children Act. A care order automatically discharges a s 8 order, s 91(2) Children Act.

- Section 9(2) states:

  No application may be made by a local authority for a residence order or contact order and no court shall make such an order in favour of a local authority.

- Section 9(3) imposes restrictions on the application to the court for leave to apply for s 8 orders by some foster parents.

  All foster parents need leave of the court to apply for a s 8 order unless they are entitled to apply. If they have fostered the child within the preceding six months they will need the consent of the local authority before seeking leave to apply unless they are related to the child, or the child has lived with them for a period exceeding three years.

- Section 9(4) goes on to provide that 'the period of three years ... need not be continuous, but must have begun not more than five years before the making of the application'.

- Section 9(5)(a) forbids a court to make a specific issue or prohibited steps order 'with a view to achieving a result which could be achieved by making a residence or contact order.'

  Specific issue and prohibited steps orders are regarded as quite formidable powers, to be used sparingly and only where appropriate.

- Section 9(5)(b) forbids a court to exercise its power to make a specific issue or prohibited steps order 'in any way which is denied to the High Court (by s 100(2)) in the exercise of its inherent jurisdiction with respect to children.'

  The essential purpose of s 100(2) Children Act is to ensure that local authorities seeking some measure of control over a child do so by way of proceedings under Parts IV or V of the Act and not by invoking wardship. Section 9(5)(b) Children Act applies the same principle to s 8 proceedings.

- Section 9(6) prohibits the making of any s 8 order which is to have effect for a period which will end after the child has reached the age of 16, unless the circumstances are exceptional. A child with severe learning difficulties or physical mobility problems may well constitute an exception.

14.3 Contact

A contact order means an order requiring the person with whom a child lives, or is to live, to allow the child to visit the person named in the order, or for that person and the child otherwise to have contact with each other.

This order governs contact by direct and indirect means, including visits, staying over, telephone calls, tapes, videos, letters, cards and presents.

Contact orders generally will expire when the child reaches 16, unless there are exceptional circumstances. Contact orders lapse if the parents live continuously together for more than six months, s 11(6) Children Act.

14.4 Prohibited steps

A prohibited steps order means an order that no step which could be taken by a parent in meeting his parental responsibility for a child, and which is of a kind specified in the order, shall be taken by any person without the consent of the court.

This order enables the court to spell out those matters which are to be referred back to it for a decision.

14.5 Residence

A residence order means an order settling the arrangements to be made as to the person with whom the child is to live.

Section 11(4) Children Act empowers the court to specify periods of residence in each household involved, and for all s 8 orders, under s 11(7), the court may make conditions and directions if necessary to facilitate the implementation of the order.

14.5.1 Residence orders and parental responsibility

Residence orders do not remove parental responsibility from anyone else who has it. Parental responsibility can be given to the person in whose favour a residence order is made, remaining while the order is in force, s 12(2) Children Act, and see Chapter 4. Residence orders generally expire when the child reaches 16, unless there are exceptional circumstances, see 14.2.3. above.

Section 12(1) specifically requires the court to make an order under s 4 giving parental responsibility to a father in favour of whom it makes a residence order if he would not otherwise have it. The court may not bring that parental responsibility order to an end while the residence order remains in force, s 12(4). There is an additional effect of the combined operation of s 12(2) and (4) for an unmarried father, which is that discharge of the residence order, or its expiry by effluxion of time will not automatically result in the discharge of his parental responsibility for his child. He continues by implication to have parental responsibility for his child until the child reaches 18, unless it is specifically discharged by court order under s 4(4).

The Act does not allow parental responsibility given under this section to cover agreement to adoption, or a s 18 Adoption Act 1976 application, nor does it permit the appointment of a guardian for the child, s 12(3) Children Act.

Section 13(1)(b) Children Act generally prohibits the removal of a child from the United Kingdom without the written consent of every person who has parental responsibility for the child, or the leave of the court; whilst s 13(2) makes an exception permitting a person in whose favour a residence order is made to take the child abroad for a period of less than one month.

A parent who fears that a child may be removed abroad permanently on the pretext of a short holiday may apply for a prohibited steps order excluding the effect of s 13(2). Where the question of the removal of the child from the jurisdiction is anticipated the court may on the making of a residence order give leave either generally, or for specified purposes, s 13(3).

Where a child is subject to a residence order or to a care order, no person may change that child's surname without the written consent of every person with parental responsibility for that child, or leave of the court, s 13(1)(a) Children Act.

14.6 Specific issue

A specific issue order means an order giving directions for the purpose of determining a specific issue which has arisen, or which may arise, in connection with any aspect of parental responsibility for a child.

This order enables either parent to submit a particular dispute to the court for resolution in accordance with the child's best interests. The order was not envisaged as a way of giving one parent the right to determine issues in advance, nor was it intended to be a substitute for a residence or contact order.

14.7 Supplementary provisions

Section 11(1) instructs the court to 'draw up a timetable with a view to determining the question without delay' and 'to give such directions as it considers appropriate for the purpose of ensuring, so far as is reasonably practicable, that the timetable is adhered to'.

Section 11(2) permits rules of court to 'specify periods within which specified steps must be taken in relation to proceedings in which such questions arise', and 'to make other provision ... for the purpose of ensuring, so far as is reasonably practicable, that such questions are determined without delay', see the Family Proceedings Courts Rules and the Family Court Rules 1991.

Section 11(4) states:

> Where a court has power to make a s 8 order, it may do so at any time in the course of the proceedings in question, even though it is not in a position to dispose finally of those proceedings.

Where a residence order is made in favour of two or more persons who do not themselves live together, the order may specify the periods during which the child is to live in the different households concerned, s 11(4).

Where there is a residence order in force, as a result of which the child lives, or is to live, with one of two parents who each have parental responsibility for him, the residence order shall cease to have effect if the parents live together for a continuous period of more than six months, s 11(5).

Section 11(6) states:

> A contact order which requires the parent with whom a child lives to allow the child to visit, or otherwise have contact with, his other parent shall cease to have effect if the parents live together for a continuous period of more than six months.

Section 8 orders may contain directions, impose conditions, be made for a specified period, or contain provisions for a specified period; and make such incidental, supplemental or consequential provisions as the court thinks fit, s 11(7).

14.8 Practice and procedure in s 8 applications

Procedure is governed in the magistrates' court by the Family Proceedings (Children Act 1989) Rules 1991, SI 1991/1395 [FP (CA) R 1991], and in the county court and High Court by the Family Proceedings Rules 1991, SI 1991/1247 [FPR 1991].

14.8.1 Applications

Freestanding applications should be on form C1, or form C2 if the application is made in existing 'family proceedings', Sched 1 FP (CA) R 1991 and App 1 FPR 1991.

If the application is for leave only, then, unless it is ex parte, the applicant for leave needs to request leave in writing and to file and serve the request together with the draft of the form C1 or C2.

14.8.2 Venue

Applications may be made at any level. Venue of hearings is governed by the Children (Allocation of Proceedings) Order 1991, SI 1991/1677; and in adoption cases, currently by the Adoption Act 1976. If children seek leave to apply for a s 8 order, the case should be heard in the High Court, under *Practice Direction (Children Act 1989 – Applications by Children)* [1993] 1 WLR 313; [1993] 1 All ER 820; [1993] 1 FLR 1008.

The legal aid board will expect that wherever possible the case is commenced in the lowest tier, the family proceedings court, and will seek justification of commencement elsewhere. If there are factors which justify transfer up, see Chapter 15.

14.8.3 Notice of application for s 8 orders

Under r 4(3) and Sched 2 Col (iv) FP (CA) R 1991 and r 4.4(3) App 3 Col (iv) FPR 1991, notice shall be served on:

- any local authority providing accommodation for the child;
- anyone with whom the child is living when proceedings commence;
- any person providing refuge in which child is staying;
- any person named in court order, still in effect, relating to child;
- any party to pending proceedings relating to the child;
- every person with whom applicant believes child has lived for three years prior to the application.

Notice of the proceedings is on form C6A, giving the date, time and venue of the hearing. It should be served at least 14 days before the hearing, r 4(3) FP (CA) R 1991 and r 4.4(3) FPR 1991.

14.8.4 Respondents

Under r 7(1) and Sched 2 Col (iii) FP (CA) R 1991 and r 4.7(1) and App 3 Col (iii) FPR 1991, the following are automatically respondents to a s 8 application:

- everyone with parental responsibility for the child;
- if a care order is in force, everyone with parental responsibility when the order was made;
- parties to proceedings leading to an order for which variation or discharge is now sought.

Respondents should be served with a copy of the application with the date of hearing endorsed on it, together with notice of the proceedings on form C6A. It should be served at least 14 days before the hearing, r 4(1)(b) and Sched 2 col (ii) FP (CA) R 1991 and r 4.4(1)(b) App 3 Col (ii) FPR 1991, as amended.

Anyone may apply on form C2 to be joined as respondent, or may be made a respondent by court order without application, see r 7(2) and (5) and FP (CA) R 1991 and Rules 4.7(2) and (5) FPR 1991. The same applies if respondents wish to be removed. If the person requesting party status has parental responsibility for the child, the court must grant their request, r 7(4) FP (CA) R 1991 and r 4.7(4) FPR 1991.

14.8.5 Service

Service can be carried out by delivery to the solicitor acting for the person to be served, personally, by document exchange, facsimile transmission, or by first class post; or by delivery to the person himself either personally or by first class post to his last known residence, r 8(1)(a) and (b) FP (CA) R 1991 and r 4.8(1)(a) and (b) FPR 1991.

The court has the power under the rules to abridge, waive or vary the manner of service, r 8(8) FP (CA) R 1991 and r 4.8(8) FPR 1991.

14.8.6 *Ex parte* procedures

Applications for s 8 orders may be made *ex parte* in any court, r 4(4)(a) FP (CA) R 1991 and r 4.4(4)(a) FPR 1991 but applicants will need leave of the justices clerk in the family proceedings court, r 4(4)(i) FP (CA) R 1991.

Ex parte applications must be supported by the same forms (C1 or C2) which should be brought to court or, if it is a telephone application, they should be filed within 24 hours of the application. In any event, they should be served on the respondents within 48 hours of any order being made. The court has the power under the rules to give directions as to service, see below.

Ex parte residence orders are frowned upon by the courts, and in a number of decisions this has been reiterated: *Re H (A Minor) (Interim Custody)* [1991 2 FLR 411; *Re G (Minors) (Ex Parte Interim Residence Order)* [1993] 1 FLR 910; *Re P (A Minor) (Ex Parte Interim Residence Order)* [1993] 1 FLR 915.

Basically, *ex parte* residence orders should be reserved for extreme urgency, such as child abduction cases. The court referral procedures for urgent applications are set out in a circular from the Lord Chancellor's Department, 'Guide to Listing Officers', September 1991.

14.8.7 Withdrawal, variation, discharge and appeals

Leave of the court is necessary for withdrawal of s 8 applications (r 5 FP (CA) R 1991 and r 4.5 FPR 1991) on oral application where the guardian *ad litem* and the parties are present; or by written request, setting out the reasons for withdrawal, which must then be duly served. The court may permit withdrawal without a hearing if the parties have had a chance to make representations to it and the views of the guardian *ad litem* or court welfare officer have been canvassed, and it is appropriate. The court may direct that a date be set for hearing the application on seven days' notice to the parties and the guardian *ad litem* or court welfare officer.

Applications to vary or discharge a s 8 order may be made by those entitled to seek the original order (see 14.1-2 above, and applications at 14.8). The procedure is the same as the original application. Under s 91(14) Children Act, the court may order that no further application be made without leave.

Section 8 orders are automatically discharged by the making of a care order, or an adoption order, see s 91(2) Children Act.

An appeal may be lodged with the High Court under s 94(1) Children Act against a decision of a family proceedings court concerning a s 8 order. Appeals against decisions made in the county court and High Court follow the general rules, and lie to the Court of Appeal. See Chapter 17 below.

14.9 Family assistance order

Section 16 Children Act creates the family assistance order, requiring a probation or local authority officer to be made available to 'advise, assist and befriend' any person named in the order, s 16(1). But note that the court can only make this order where the circumstances are exceptional, or the court has the consent of every person named in the order save the child, s 16(3).

The person to be 'advised assisted or befriended' may be the child, or his or her parent or guardian, or any person with whom the child is living or who has a contact order in respect of the child, s 16(2). It lasts for six months, or a shorter specified period, s 16(5).

The family assistance order may direct the person(s) named in the order to take whatever steps are necessary to enable the officer to be kept informed of their address, and to be allowed to visit the named person, s 16(4).

Where there is in force a family assistance order and also a s 8 order, then the officer may refer to the court the possibility of variation or discharge of the s 8 order, s 16(6). This power should obviously be of use where a family assistance order has been made at the same time as a contact order which is clearly not working.

14.10 Order to local authority to investigate under s 37 Children Act

Where, in any 'family proceedings', see s 8(3) Children Act, in which a question arises with respect to the welfare of any child, it appears to the court that it may be appropriate for a care or supervision order to be made the court may direct the appropriate authority to undertake an investigation of the child's circumstances, s 37(1) Children Act.

The local authority to whom the direction is given is then under a duty to consider whether it should:
- apply for a care or supervision order;
- provide services or assistance for the child and family;
- take any other action in respect of the child.

If the local authority decides not to seek a care order, it shall inform the court within eight weeks from the s 37 direction of its reasons, any services or assistance provided, and any other action taken. If the decision is made to seek care or supervision, the local authority shall also consider whether it would be appropriate to review the case at a later date, and the date of any such review shall be determined.

15 Commencement and Transfer of Proceedings

15.1 General rules

The general rule is that private law applications under the Children Act 1989 (the 'Children Act') may be made at any level of the court, subject to the restrictions of the Legal Aid Board, which, of course, wishes to keep costs down.

In public law cases, the general rule is that proceedings should be commenced in the family proceedings court, with certain exceptions.

A checklist of basic commencement provisions is set out at Figure 18 (pp 120-21).

The venue of hearings under the Children Act and the Adoption Act 1976 is governed by the Children (Allocation of Proceedings) Order 1991, SI 1991/1677; the Children (Allocation of Proceedings) (Appeals) Order 1991, SI 1991/1801; the Family Proceedings (Amendment) Rules 1991, SI 1991/2113; and reference may also be made to the Home Office Circular 45/91 (in the Children Act 1989 *Guidance and Regulations*, Vol 7 at p 114).

The county courts are divided into categories, each having the power to hear specified types of case. These are **Care Centres**, **Family Hearing Centres**, and also **Divorce Centres**. It is also important to ascertain that the court in which the case is to be heard is appropriate.

In addition, it is vital to ensure that the judge has power to deal with the case. This is referred to colloquially as having a 'ticket' for the type of proceedings, eg ' a care ticket'. To check whether a case is appropriate for a category of judge, refer to the *Family Proceedings (Allocation to Judiciary) Directions 1993* [1993] 2 FLR 1008.

15.2 Specified exceptions to the general rules

Public law proceedings may be commenced in the county court or the High Court if:

- there are proceedings pending in another court;
- there has been a court-directed investigation into the child's circumstances;
- the application is for extension, variation or discharge of an existing order. In these circumstances the application may be made to the court in which the proceedings are pending, or the existing order was made.

Certain proceedings need to be heard at High Court level, and these are discussed in the text as they arise. Most arise through case law, and include applications for authorisation of the use of blood products where there is religious objection, leave to submit a child to HIV tests, cases with an international issue and restriction of general publicity issues.

If a child seeks leave to apply for a s 8 order, the case should be heard in the High Court, under *Practice Direction (Children Act 1989 – Applications by Children)* [1993] 1 WLR 313; [1993] 1 All ER 820; [1993] 1 FLR 1008.

15.3 Transfers

Transfers are governed generally by the Children (Allocation of Proceedings) Order 1991, SI 1991/1677.

When proceedings are commenced in one level of the court, they may be transferred up or down the tiers if necessary, subject to the restrictions on venue outlined above. The Children Act Advisory Committee produced a list of 'Transfer Triggers' see Chapter 8, figure 12, p 64.

These are factors the presence of one or more of which in a case may be persuasive to the court to transfer the matter up. When transferring a case, the court must have regard to the principles in s 1 Children Act, and in particular the avoidance of delay. There is an excellent section for reference on transfers in *Family Law, Children Law and Practice*, Hershman and MacFarlane, Vol 1 at D 61-137.

Figure 18: Commencement of proceedings

Children Act 1989 Section	Order	Applicant	Needs leave	Form	Court can make order of own volition	Family Proceedings Court	County Court	High Court
4	Parental Responsibility	Child's Father		C1 or C2		Children (Allocation of Proceedings) Order 1991 SI 1991/1677 & Home Office Circular 45/91		
4(3)	Termination of PR	Person with PR Child		C1 or C2		Applicant's Choice, subject to legal aid restrictions	Applicant's Choice, subject to legal aid restrictions	
5	Appoint Guardian	Anyone	✓	C1 or C2		Applicant's Choice, subject to legal aid restrictions	Applicant's Choice, subject to legal aid restrictions	
6	Terminate appt of Guardian	Anyone with PR Child	✓	C1 or C2		Applicant's Choice, subject to legal aid restrictions	Applicant's Choice, subject to legal aid restrictions	
8	Contact	Parent / Guardian / Person with Residence Order / Party to marriage / Person with care of child for 3 years or consent of those with PR	Anyone with leave may apply	C1 or C2	✓	Applicant's Choice, subject to legal aid restrictions	Applicant's Choice, subject to legal aid restrictions	– Child's Application for Leave
8	Residence	Parent / Guardian / Person with Residence Order / Party to marriage / Person with care of child for 3 years or consent of those with PR	Anyone with leave may apply	C1 or C2	✓	Applicant's Choice, subject to legal aid restrictions	Applicant's Choice, subject to legal aid restrictions	– Child's Application for Leave
8	Prohibited Steps	Parent / Guardian / Person with Residence Order	* Anyone with leave may apply	C1 or C2	✓	Applicant's Choice, subject to legal aid restrictions	Applicant's Choice, subject to legal aid restrictions	– Child's Application for Leave / – HIV Tests / – Restriction of Publicity / – International dimension / – Use of Blood Products

15.4 Urgent applications

The court referral procedures for urgent applications are set out in a circular from the Lord Chancellor's Department 'Guide to Listing Officers', September 1991.

Initially, if the matter can be handled by a nominated judge at the local court then it should be. As a general rule, circuits should deal with matters arising on Friday evenings, weekends, public and privilege holidays. The Royal Courts of Justice will take cases during weekday evenings and nights, and also be available as a longstop for the circuit arrangements at weekends and public and privilege holidays.

The out of hours contact number of the Royal Courts of Justice is 0171 936 6000. The security officer will, on request, refer the caller to the urgent business officer for the day.

The urgent business officer needs to know:
- the type of application;
- circumstances of the case.

He will decide whether the case merits contacting one of the three members of the judiciary on duty, at the appropriate level, and he will then return the call within 10-15 minutes. The judge dealing with the matter will advise on how the application should be handled.

COMMENCEMENT AND TRANSFER OF PROCEEDINGS 121

	Specific Issue	Applicant	Form		Applicant's Choice, subject to legal aid restrictions / Any Court	
8	Specific Issue	Parent, Guardian, Person with Residence Order	C1 or C2			– Child seeks Leave & able child disabled – Blood Products use – HIV Tests – Restriction of Publicity – International dimension
		*Anyone with leave may apply				
16	Family Assistance Order	Can only be made on the courts' volition with consent of the parties		✓		
25	Secure Accommodation	Local Authority, Area Health Auth. NHS Trust, Person caring in a residential home	C1 + Supplement C20	✓	✓ E	E = EXCEPTIONS: * Court directed investigations * Pending Proceedings
31	Care Order or Supervision Order	Local Authority or NSPCC	C1, C2 + Suppl. C13		✓ E	* Extension variation or discharge of existing order
34	Care Contact Order	Local Authority, Child, Anyone with leave	C1 or C2	Court can make s 34 order along with Care Order	✓ E	may be commenced in the court in which direction given, proceedings are pending, or original order was made
36	Education Supervision Order	Local Education Authority	Form C17 or C17A		✓ E	
43	Child Assessment Order	Local Authority or NSPCC	C1 + Suppl. C16		✓ E	
44	Emergency Protection	Any Person	C1 with Suppl. C11		✓ E	
50	Recovery Order	Person with PR by care order or Emergency Protection order, Designated Officer	C1 with Suppl. C18		✓ E	

16 Working with Children

16.1 Role of the guardian *ad litem*

An important function of the guardian *ad litem* is to interview all those who may be able to give relevant information about the child's life and circumstances, and also the child and her family. The guardian *ad litem* has a duty to advise the court of the child's wishes and feelings; to inform the court of the child's circumstances, bearing in mind the welfare check list; to evaluate all the options open to the court; and finally to advise the court on the best way forward in the interests of the child.

The provisions governing the appointment and functioning of a guardian *ad litem* are in ss 41-42 Children Act 1989 (the 'Children Act'), and r 10 Family Proceedings Court (Children Act) Rules 1991, SI 1991/1395, and r 4.10 Family Proceedings Rules 1991, SI 1991/1247.

The guardian *ad litem* has access under s 42(1) Children Act to all social work files and records, and if any of these documents are copied by the guardian *ad litem*, they are admissible in evidence before the court, s 42 (2). See the case of *Re T* [1994] 1 FLR 632 in which the local authority refused to disclose records of potential adopters to the guardian *ad litem*. The Court of Appeal held that the case records of adoption were within the definition of the documents to which the guardian *ad litem* should have access under the terms of s 42 Children Act.

Note the recent leading case of *Oxfordshire County Council v P* [1995] 1 FLR 582 concerning the issue of how confidential information should be treated by guardians *ad litem*.

The guardian *ad litem* may ask for access to medical or psychiatric records of the child, and may wish to see the health records of others involved in the child's life. The Court of Appeal in the case of *Oxfordshire County Council v M* [1994] 1 FLR 175 set a precedent for disclosure of psychiatric reports (even if unfavourable to the commissioning party) to all those involved in child protection cases. It is submitted that this principle should now be extended in the interests of the child to the disclosure of verbal comment, and also of other expert reports, the content of which is of relevance to the welfare of the child.

Under s 41(1) Children Act, a guardian *ad litem* shall be appointed for the purpose of 'specified proceedings' unless the court is satisfied that it is not necessary to do so in order to safeguard the child's interests.

Figure 19: Specified proceedings

Specified proceedings are defined in s 41(6) Children Act as:

(a) care or supervision order applications;

(b) where court has given s 37 directions and is considering whether to make care or supervision order;

(c) application for discharge of care order or variation or discharge of supervision order;

(d) application under s 39(4) for substitution of supervision order for care order by person entitled to seek discharge of care (ie child, person with parental responsibility, or designated local authority);

(e) where court is considering whether to make a residence order with respect to a child subject to a care order;

(f) care contact order (s 34);

(g) an order under Part V including:

    s 43   Child Assessment Orders;

    s 44   Emergency Protection Orders;

    s 48   Discovery Order;

    s 50   Recovery Order;

(h) appeals against:

    (i)   making or refusal to make care order, supervision order or order under s 34;

    (ii)   making or refusal to make a residence order with respect to a child subject to a care order;

    (iii)   variation or discharge, or refusal of an application to vary or discharge the orders in (i) and (ii) above;

    (iv)   refusal of an application under s 39(4);

    (v)   making or refusal to make order under Part V;

and other cases specified by FPC (Children Act) Rules 1991 r 2(1):
(a) family proceedings under s 25 (secure accommodation);
(b) applications under s 33(7) (change of surname or removal of child from jurisdiction);
(c) arrangements for child to live abroad under para 19(1) of Sched 2;
(d) applications under para 6(3) of Sched 3 by supervisor to extend supervision order.

Specified proceedings now include applications for parental orders under s 30 Human Fertilisation and Embryology Act 1990.

See also the Children Act 1989 Guidance and Regulations Vol 7 'Guardians *ad litem* and other Court-related Issues' from HMSO.

For discussion of conflict between guardian *ad litem* and child, see Chapter 13 at 13.4 above.

16.2 Should I see my child client?

Lawyers representing children should, as a matter of good practice, meet with their child clients, unless, exceptionally, there is good reason not to do so. Necessary arrangements should be made in co-operation with the guardian *ad litem*, the child's parents and carers, and the local authority.

The Law Society produced a book for solicitors who represent children, *Acting for Children* by Christine Liddle, 1992. It contains advice and information about case preparation and conduct of the child's lawyer.

At p 5 Liddle says:

> The solicitor's duty is to act on behalf of the child, but to take his instructions from the guardian *ad litem* unless the child is 'able, having regard to his understanding' to give his own instructions ... the assessment of the child's ability to give separate instructions is something that must be discussed with the guardian *ad litem*, but ultimately the solicitor has to make up his own mind and act accordingly.

Here is a source of possible misunderstanding. There is a clear distinction between the question of separate representation, and the issue of speaking with child clients generally. Legal aid in public law proceedings is granted to the child client, through the guardian *ad litem*. Initially, the solicitor is instructed through the guardian *ad litem*, but will need, as a vital part of the preparation of the case, to ascertain the wishes and feelings of the child, and to check as the case progresses whether there is any area of conflict between an older child and the guardian. The solicitor is under a duty to make the child's wishes and feelings known to the court. The guardian *ad litem* has a similar duty. Under rule 12(1)(a) Family Proceedings Court (Children Act 1989) Rules 1991, SI 1991/1395, and r 4.12(1)(a) Family Proceedings Rules 1991, SI 1991/1247, if a child radically disagrees with the guardian *ad litem*, and is able to instruct his or her own solicitor, then the court must be informed. The solicitor continues to represent the child client. The guardian *ad litem* will then proceed unrepresented, or seek another lawyer where necessary.

Solicitors will need to speak with child clients who appear to be of sufficient maturity to discover, firstly, whether the child is sufficiently mature to instruct separately if necessary, and, secondly, whether a conflict exists between the child and the guardian *ad litem*. The solicitor also needs to elicit the child's wishes and feelings in order to represent them to the court.

In Christine Liddle's book it is assumed that the lawyer and the guardian *ad litem* will work in conjunction with each other, and that both the lawyer and the guardian *ad litem* will be meeting child clients. At p 5 she states: 'As the case progresses, he (the solicitor) should discuss which written information should be disclosed to the child, and which one of them should do it.' Later, at p 6, she says specifically: 'Although children vary in their ability to give instructions, it is still very beneficial to the solicitor's understanding of the case for him to meet his child client, whatever the age.'

If a solicitor is to represent a child properly in court, it is necessary to understand the child's personality, behaviour, background and needs. This can be done through information gained by others, but it is best done at first hand. Even a small baby can non-verbally tell the observer a good deal about herself. Seeing a child in his environment and interacting with him gives not only greater understanding of the child but also a sense of involvement with the client which makes the task so much more personal, and gives encouragement to the solicitor act for the child as a person, rather than as an 'object of concern' or 'a case'.

In October 1994, the Solicitors Family Law Committee produced *Guidance for Solicitors Acting for Children in Private Law Proceedings under the Children Act 1989*. This *Guidance* comments that:

A solicitor's professional training is not well designed to equip him or her to make an assessment of a child's understanding unaided, although solicitors, particularly those on the Children Panel, will have a certain amount of knowledge through experience and/or will have undergone some training in child development.

Clearly, the expectation is that solicitors will at least discuss the issue of competence with the experts in the case, and this principle should apply equally in public law cases. The guardian *ad litem* in a public law case is the first person to be consulted on the issue. Child psychologists, psychiatrists, counsellors and others working with the child will also have useful views.

'*Gillick* competence' as evolved from the case of *Gillick v West Norfolk and Wisbech Health Authority and DSS* [1986] AC 112 followed by the later cases of *Re S* [1993] 2 FLR 437, *Re CT* [1993] 2 FLR 278, *Re H (Minor) (Care Proceedings: Child's wishes)* [1993] 1 FLR 440 and *Re M* [1994] 1 FLR 749 is vitally important. The Law Society refers also to 'The Child as Client' by Philip King and Ian Young, *Family Law*, 1992, with approval.

In the *Guide to Good Practice for Solicitors Acting for Children*, 2nd edn, 1995, from the Solicitors Family Law Association, there is a section 'Seeing the child' which states at E para 1:

> When acting for a child, the solicitor should always meet the child and due regard should be taken for the most appropriate setting and style for such a meeting. Interviews should be short and at the child's pace.

'The guardian *ad litem*' by Pat Monro and Lis Forrester, *Family Law*, 1995, examines the role of the guardian *ad litem*, and the representation of children. The authors assume that solicitors will meet their child clients, and they add practical advice on how to go about this:

> Where a young child is involved, the instructions will come from the guardian *ad litem* and it will usually be appropriate for the guardian *ad litem* to meet with the child in the first instance without the solicitor, who can be introduced at a later date. A young child will probably be confused by the introduction of a number of new faces, and therefore it is important for the guardian *ad litem* to get to know the child before the solicitor becomes involved.

There are very rare cases where it may be inappropriate for the solicitor to see the child, for example where the child is severely emotionally damaged and the introduction of a new face may adversely affect his therapeutic progress.

16.3 Taking instructions and communicating with children

A solicitor needs to be able to communicate with children if instructions are to be effective. A basic understanding of child development, confidence in being with children (preferably accrued with practical experience), and integrity are vital. Children dislike being patronised, and they will see through prevarication. They deserve the respect of straight answers to their questions in age appropriate language.

It is good to write to older child clients to let them know that they have a solicitor and to provide a channel of communication which they can take up themselves if they are worried or curious about anything. A few stamped envelopes addressed to the solicitor's office sent with the introductory letter enable the child to write back if she wishes. It also empowers her: she will not be reliant on others to get in touch with her solicitor. Some solicitors will provide a phone card for older children. Many younger children like to send their solicitor a drawing if they can't write back, and to have their own letter back is a great boost for their confidence. Space is needed in the office for the drawings that will inevitably accumulate!

Everyone has his own way of communicating with others, so there are no hard and fast rules, but figure 20 below gives a few guidelines.

Figure 20: Communication with children

- Discuss the timing of the first meeting with the child with the guardian *ad litem*, and whether to go with them on the first visit to the child.
- Find out what the guardian has already told the child about the case and about the role of guardian and solicitor, and how much of the facts it is appropriate to tell the child or to discuss with her.
- Explain clearly and honestly issues of confidentiality to the child in age-appropriate language.
- Children do not like being being patronised.
- Informal clothing is best, not formal or intimidating 'power dressing' clothes.
  Solicitors may sit on the floor to talk/play with young clients!

- Take a few props to help communication: a selection from these may be useful: paper, crayons or pencils (never felt tips or your best fountain pen), pipe cleaners, a glove puppet, a few small toys, a family of dolls, car, toy telephone, etc.
- Usually, the guardian will have introduced the solicitor to the child, but if not, then, once the child is at ease, explain in simple language what a child's solicitor's job involves. For an older child it could be something like this:

  > I am your solicitor. Part of my job is to go to the court and talk to the judge (or magistrates) and to tell the judge what you want to happen, and how you feel about what is happening to you. I need to get to know you, and you can tell me what you want me to say to the judge.

  There will be much more to explain and discuss with a child client, but this is a start!
- What does the child wish to be called? Names are important. Does the child have preferred names for himself or others?
- Try to understand the child, get him to talk about his favourite television programme, food, colours, football team, toys, friends, and pets.
- Explain to the child what the proceedings are, in an age appropriate way.
- Don't overtire a young child, or overstay: an hour or less is usually enough.
- Don't try to press a child for facts, or get them into an emotional state which their carers then have to deal with afterwards. Keep them calm and their emotions as even as possible. Solicitors are not expected to be experts at communication with children. Involve the child's carers if help is needed to engage the child; and end the visit if the child seems unwilling to continue. Never distress a child by being 'pushy' if they do not want to talk, or by overstaying. The guardian *ad litem* will assist with advice, help or, if the solicitor is unsure, a joint visit to the child can be made.
- A sense of calm, goodwill and appropriate humour helps!

16.4 Child development

There is not space in this book to discuss child development in any detail. There are a number of excellent reference books on the market, some of which are listed in Chapter 19 below. *The Orange Book: Protecting Children – A Guide to Social Workers Undertaking a Comprehensive Assessment*, HMSO, contains several pages of information on child development at pp 88–93. This, together with a reference book often used by guardians *ad litem Child Development – Diagnosis and Assessment* by KS Holt, Butterworth Heinemann, 1994, would prove sufficient for most situations.

The *ABC of One to Seven*, published by the BMJ is useful, and many book shops carry a range of books on child development intended for parents which practitioners will find readable and helpful.

16.5 Understanding your child client – race, religion, culture and ethnicity

The welfare checklist pays attention to the child's 'physical educational and emotional needs', s 1(3)(b) Children Act; and 'age, sex, background and any characteristics of his which the court considers relevant', s 1(3)(d) Children Act.

Although the Children Act did not refer specifically to race, religion and culture, they are clearly included in these categories. If the child's background, and needs arising from it, is not clear to the solicitor and guardian *ad litem*, then expert assistance should be sought from someone who fully understands the child's cultural, religious and social needs. The child may also have physical needs which may have to be explained to a carer from a different culture, eg food, religious taboos and customs, hair and skin care, etc. Quite often, behaviour which would not make sense within one culture in a given situation makes perfect sense when understood in the context of another. The court must take the child's needs fully into account when deciding the most appropriate way forward to promote and safeguard the child's welfare.

16.6 After the case is over

Children often develop a relationship of trust with their solicitor, and, whatever the outcome of the case, will frequently keep in touch. The guardian *ad litem*'s role for the child ceases when the final order is made.

By contrast, the solicitor is a continuing source of help, and a useful contact in the outside world. Children will be pleased to have their own solicitor whom they can telephone or ask about problems as they arise, particularly as they reach their teenage years.

It is good to have a final visit to a child client, and to let them have a business card to keep if they are old enough to use it. A few sheets of blank paper and a few stamped envelopes addressed to the solicitor can be left with the child, in case they want to write. If a child does write, or otherwise make contact, make a point of responding immediately, and in a way appropriate for the child's age and understanding.

Children who are in care need to know their rights, and these should have been explained by the social services department. If a child is concerned about the standard of care, or has a need to complain, the solicitor may be the first person they think of to tell about their problem. Older children may at some time wish to instruct a solicitor on their own behalf to apply for a s 8 order, or to apply to discharge a care order, so it is essential to keep an avenue of communication open for them.

Often the child may be concerned about an aspect of their care, and the solicitor can perform a useful function in explaining and mediating between the child and parents or agencies when difficulties arise.

Older children on leaving care also have the right to additional services on leaving care under s 24 Children Act, and they may wish to seek advice about the ways in which their needs can be met.

Case records, statements and documents should be kept at least until the child reaches 21. In adoption cases, records may need to be kept longer. Check with the local panel of guardians *ad litem* on their recommendations. Guardians working from home may rely on the solicitor or their panel office to store papers. It goes without saying that cases are confidential and need to be kept securely.

17 Legal Aid, Appeals and Enforcement

17.1 Legal aid

There is insufficient space here to discuss legal aid issues in detail, but the *Legal Aid Handbook*, published by Sweet & Maxwell, is excellent for reference. Fortunately, the new legal aid forms in child and family proceedings each have headings which indicate the proceedings to which they apply, as well as detailed instructions for completion of the form.

The child, parents and those with parental responsibility may have 'free' legal aid (non-means, non-merits tested) for care, supervision, extension or discharge of emergency protection and child assessment; and the child only for secure accommodation applications. The only formality is completion of form CLA 5A by the solicitor.

Other child and family law applications under the Children Act 1989 (the 'Children Act'), Adoption Act 1976, Child Abduction and Custody Act 1985, and the Child Support Act 1991 require form CLA 5, plus one of the means forms: CLA 4A (general), CLA 4B (for those on income support or benefit), or CLA 4F (for children under 16).

Emergency applications may be made to the Legal Aid Board by telephone or post, and must be supported by the appropriate forms, plus form CLA 3 sent in immediately thereafter.

Expert witnesses need prior authority, on form CLA 31, and amendments on form CLA 30.

Note that parties to applications to discharge care orders, and parties other than the child in secure accommodation applications are not covered by the 'free' legal aid, and have to complete CLA 5 and a means form.

17.2 Appeals and judicial review

Appeals are discussed briefly in these practice notes under each topic, but since there is limited space, judicial review, complaints procedures and appeals procedures can only be mentioned, giving further references. 'Children Law and Practice', Hershman and MacFarlane, *Family Law*, has an excellent section on judicial review and appeals in Vol 1 at section 1. Other useful books are *Judicial Review Proceedings*, Jonathan Manning, Legal Action Group, 1995; the *Judicial Review Handbook*, Michael Fordham, Wiley, 1994 and the *Applicant Guide to Judicial Review*, Ed Richard Paynter, Sweet & Maxwell, 1995.

17.2.1 Family proceedings court appeals to the High Court

There is no 'slip rule', and no power to review or rehear a decision. What is pronounced by the chair of the Bench must be written up as the order, and amendment can only happen if the words are not accurately written down. Orders are challenged by notice of appeal within 7 days of interim care or supervision orders, or 14 days otherwise, or by way of case stated to the High Court under s 94(1) Children Act, Ord 55 r 1(1)(2) Rules of the Supreme Court and r 4.22 Family Proceedings Rules 1991, SI 1991/1247.

17.2.2 County court appeals

Appeal lies from decisions of the district judge to a judge of the same court, r 4.22 (4) Family Proceedings Rules 1991.

The county court has the power to review interim, ex parte, or interlocutory orders; or to rehear its own decisions where there has been no error of the court. In other cases there may be an application to discharge the order, or the parties may serve notice of appeal within 14 days of the decision to the Court of Appeal, and are governed by Ord 59 Rules of the Supreme Court.

17.2.3 High Court appeals

Appeal lies from decisions of a district judge to a judge of the same court, for rehearing, no leave required, Ord 58 r 1 Rules of the Supreme Court.

The High Court has the power to review interim, ex parte, or interlocutory orders; or to rehear its own decisions where there has been no error of the court, s 17 Supreme Court Act. In other cases there may be an application to discharge the order, or the parties may serve

Figure 21: Table of enforcement procedures for Children Act orders

Breach of Order	Injunction/Penal Notice	Surety Bond	Committal or Contempt	Other Remedy Available	Police Powers and Criminal Proceedings
Refusal to give up a child for Residence Order			RSC Ord 45 r 7 CCR Ord 29 r 1 High Court or county court may commit Family Proc Court may use s 63(3) MCA 1980	Search and Recovery Order s 34 Family Law Reform Act 1986	
Threat to remove child from UK, or actual removal attempt		can be used to ensure return of child	as above	'Seek & Find' High Court Inherent jurisdiction	1) Police duty to assist where threat of danger or breach of the peace 2) Child Abduction & Custody Act 1985 Offence
Change of name when child subject to residence order, w/o consent or leave	✓			1) Port Alert System 2) Passport Restriction	
Refusal to comply with s 8 Contact Order	To use penal notice the acts to be enforced must be set out clearly in the order		Committal is rare, but possible	s 34 Family Law Reform Act 1986 possible, combined with s 11(7) directions	
Breach of specific issue or prohibited steps	✓		✓		Police duty to assist where threat of danger may be used in medical emergency

Removal of child from care (under s 31 order)	If removal from jurisdiction is threatened	Port Alert if threat to remove from UK High Court Tipstaff if threat to remove from jurisdiction Recovery order s 50 Children Act 1989
Chance of name of child in s 31 care without leave/consent	✓	Child Abduction & Custody Act 1985 offence Police duty to assist where threat of danger may be used in medical emergency
Failure to produce records to guardian *ad litem* in care/supervision proceedings	Application to produce documents under s 42 Children Act 1989	Application to court to produce documents under s 42 Children Act 1989
Breach of directions of the court in Children Act 1989 proceedings, as to filing, service or attendance		• Wasted Costs Order • Court may impose adjournment, or proceed in absence of party • Evidence may be disallowed – but rare in Children Act cases

notice of appeal within 14 days of the decision to the Court of Appeal. Procedure is governed by Ord 59 Rules of the Supreme Court.

Occasionally, appeals may 'leapfrog' by certificate granted under s 12(1) Administration of Justice Act 1969 direct to the House of Lords.

17.3 Complaints procedures

If any person wishes to complain about any action by the Department of Social Services in relation to a child, the procedure is set out in the Representations Procedure (Children) Regulations 1991, S1 1991/ 894. The policies which underpin the rights of 'service users', and the way in which complaints should be handled are set out in Vols 1-9 of the *Children Act 1989 Guidance and Regulations*, 'Principles and Practice in Regulations and Guidance', 1991, HMSO; and 'The Right to Complain' by the Department of Health and Social Services Inspectorate, 1991, HMSO.

17.4 Enforcement

Enforcement of orders made under the Children Act is discussed briefly in these practice notes under each topic. Further detail is available from 'Children Law and Practice', Hershman and MacFarlane, *Family Law*, which has an excellent section on enforcement of Children Act orders in Vol 1, part D section 8. (See figure 21, Table of enforcement procedures for Children Act orders, pp 134-35.)

18 Expert Evidence

18.1 Instructing experts

An expert witness is one who is accepted by the court as an expert in her specialist field.

Wall J, in the course of proceedings in the High Court, has given helpful guidance in his judgments on the use of expert witnesses, and his comments in two cases in particular – *Re M (Minors) (Care Proceedings: Childrens' Wishes)* [1994] 1 FLR 749 and *Re G (Minors) (Expert Witnesses)* [1994] 2 FLR 291 – should be compulsory reading. He sets out carefully and in detail the way in which experts are to be approached, his views on disclosure, the drafting of instructions, and the filing of the subsequent reports.

Figure 22: Expert instruction checklist

- Discuss instruction of expert with other parties, try to agree joint experts wherever possible.
- Ensure all necessary leave for disclosure wherever is obtained.
- Obtain consents for examinations and assessments.
- Co-operate on timing of conferences, reports and evidence.
- Instructions should set out context in which opinion sought.
- Instructions should define specific questions expert is to address.
- File letter of instruction with list of accompanying documents.
- Provide expert with all relevant information.
- Update expert on developments relevant to their opinion.
- Encourage co-operation between parties and experts.
- Objectivity – experts should not be biased in any way.
- Invite experts to confer together, identify areas of agreement and disputed issues.
- Do not attempt to influence or 'edit' expert reports.
- Reports must be disclosed to all parties and the court.

Figure 23: Format for expert reports in Children Act Proceedings

[Reports should carry at the top right hand side, this information:-]

Initials & surname.......
Statement No.............
Date...........................
Filed on behalf of........

[It is useful to head the report/statement in a way which identifies the court and the proceedings for which the statement is intended eg:-]

In the .... Court

Case Reference No ....

Re ....

Report of Dr ....

Date ....

Re .... *[child or children's name(s) and date(s) of birth (but not current address unless specifically authorised to disclose it)]*

[The final paragraph should be worded to comply with the requirements of the Rules, eg:-]

'I.................................. (Full name) declare that the content of this statement is true to the best of my knowledge, information, and belief; and I understand that this statement may be placed before the court.'

Signed...................................

Dated....................................

[Governed by r 4.17 Family Proceedings Rules 1991
and
r 17 Family Proceedings Court (Children Act 1989) Rules 1991]

18.2 Finances

Fees for expert witnesses can be authorised in advance by the Legal Aid Board using form CLA 31. Obtain requisite leave and consents first, together with an estimate of the cost involved, based on an hourly rate of charge, and a daily or half-daily rate for court attendance, with estimated travel or other incidental expenses. The Board will at its discretion pay unauthorised fees, but don't rely on it. The British Medical Association has offered guidance on appropriate fees. Write to an expert confirming the instructions and LAB agreed fees, and ask him to let you know when the limit of agreed costs is reached; then obtain a further extension of legal aid.

18.3 Finding the right expert

The most effective way of finding experts is recommendation by other legal practitioners in similar work. Ask expert(s) to disclose qualifications, current work and relevant past experience – not only for reassurance, but also because to do so is useful for the court, other parties and the legal aid board. Ask how often the expert has given evidence in court before – they may be brilliant on paper, but terrible at giving oral evidence. The list of registers and directories below at figure 24 may be a starting point in the search for the right expert.

Figure 24: Experts lists, registers and directories

Some of these organisations will send out published lists. Others provide information in response to a telephone or written enquiry, and may charge an administration fee.

ORGANISATION	TITLE
British Psychological Society	Directory of Chartered Psychologists
The Forensic Science Society	World List of Forensic Science Laboratories and Practices
The Forensic Science Society	Register of Independent Consultants
JS Publications	UK Register of Expert Witnesses

Law Society	Expert Witness Register
British Academy of Experts	Register of Experts

JOURNALS AND SUPPLEMENTS

Expert Evidence (International Digest of Human Behaviour, Science and Law)	SLE Publications
Solicitors Journal	Expert Witnesses Supplement
Law Society Gazette	Expert Witness Supplement

LAWYERS' LISTS

Law Society Children Panel	Membership List
London Criminal Courts Solicitors Association	Agency & Membership List
Association of Lawyers for Children	Experts database Agency database

USEFUL INFORMATION ON INSTRUCTING EXPERTS

Title	Publisher & Author
Professionals and the Courts	Carson D, Venture Press
The Expert Witness	Graham Hall J and Smith G, Barry Rose
Expert Witnesses	Jones C, Clarendon Press
The Courts and the Doctor	Gee DJ and Mason JK, Oxford University Press
Expert Evidence Law & Practice	Hodgkinson T, Sweet & Maxwell
Forensic Medicine for Lawyers	Mason JK, Butterworth

19 Information, Guidance and Reference Works

19.1 Essential information library

All Volumes of the *Children Act 1989 Guidance and Regulations* (see Chapter 1 at 1.4)

Working Together Under the Children Act 1989, HMSO, ISBN 0-11-321472-3

Protecting Children, (the 'Orange Book'), HMSO, ISBN 0-11-321159-7

Local Area Child Protection Committee Manual (obtainable from the ACPC Chair)

Children Act Advisory Committee Directions Pro Forma, CAAC

A Child & Family Law Reference Work, regularly updated (see the booklist below)

ABC of Child Abuse, ed Prof Roy Meadow (new edition), 1996, British Medical Journal

ABC of One to Seven, HB Valman, 1993 *British Medical Journal*

The Report of the Inquiry into Child Abuse in Cleveland, 1987, HMSO

Book on Child Development (see the booklist below)

Sample set of Sheffield Centile Charts with accompanying notes (obtainable from a GP or Health Visitor)

List(s) of expert witnesses

Law Reports

Journals/Newsletters

19.2 Reading and reference list

LOOSE LEAF REFERENCE WORKS

The Family Law Service, General Editor PM Bromley, Butterworths, Three volumes

Children; Law and Practice, edited by David Hershman and Andrew McFarlane, Family Law

Practical Matrimonial Precedents, edited by Clark, Parker & Blair, Longman

The Encyclopaedia of Social Services and Child Care Law, edited by Richard M Jones, Sweet & Maxwell

CHILD LAW BOOKS

The Child as Client by Philip King and Ian Young, Family Law, 1992

Acting for Children by Christine Liddle, The Law Society, 1992

The Guardian ad Litem by Pat Monro and Lis Forrester, Family Law, 1995

The Directory of Child Rights and Welfare by Clare Brennan, Prentice-Hall

The Directory for Disabled People, 7th edn compiled by Ann Darnbrough and Derek Kinrade, Prentice-Hall

Crimes Against Children by Jean Graham Hall and Douglas Martin, Barry Rose

The Children Act Manual by Judith Masson & Michael Morris, Sweet & Maxwell

Working with Children and the Children Act by Martin Herbert, The British Psychological Society

Child Abuse by Christina Lyon and Peter de Cruz, Family Law

Child Care Law by Hugh Howard and Paul Tain, Cavendish Publishing

A Practical Approach to Family Law by J Black, J Bridge and T Bond, Blackstone Press

Facing Physical Violence by Glynnis Breakwell, Routledge

The Family and School by Dowling and Osborne, Routledge

Sexuality in Adolescence by S Moore and D Rosenthal, Routledge

Re-Focus on Child Abuse edited by Alan Levy QC, Hawkesmere

Listening to Children, NSPCC

Investigating Child Abuse, NSPCC

Children's Representation, A Practitioner's Guide by Judith E Timms, Sweet & Maxwell

The National Standards for Probation Service Family Court Welfare Work from the Home Office

Significant Harm edited by Margaret Adcock, Richard White and Anne Hollows, Significant Publications

FORENSIC INVESTIGATION OF CHILD ABUSE

Beyond Blame by P Reder, S Duncan and M Gray, Hawkesmere

ABC of Child Abuse edited by Prof Roy Meadow, British Medical Association

Poppies on the Rubbish Heap — Sexual Abuse, The Child's Voice by Madge Bray, Canongate

Children as Witnesses edited by Helen Dent and Rhona Flin, Wiley

Memorandum of Good Practice in Interviewing Child Witnesses, HMSO

CHILD DEVELOPMENT

Baby & Child Birth to Age 5 by Penelope Leach, Penguin

Child Development, Diagnosis and Assessment by KS Holt, Butterworth Heinemann

EMERGENCY REMEDIES

Emergency Procedures (A Guide to Child Protection and Domestic Violence) by Nicola Wyld and Nancy Carlton, LAG

Emergency Remedies and Procedures by Nigel Fricker, JDR Adams, Nasreen Pearce, David Salter, Robert Stevens and Jonathan Whybrow, Family Law

COMPUTER SOFTWARE

CHIAC software package on child abuse, Family Law

It was developed at the University of Bath for social workers and has been in use since 1988. The four CHIAC databases are legal, medical, research studies and good practice. The medical material gives a glossary of medical terms and explanations of their meaning, eg fractures caused by physical abuse. The research studies give summaries of the findings cited together with background information and provide useful reference material, with evaluation of the research by the CHIAC team based on sampling, techniques etc, which would be helpful to Panel members in the preparation of cases and assessment of research cited by other parties.

Family Law a new Justis CD Rom from Context, London, tel 0171 267 8989. Full text of Family Law reports since 1980 on CD Rom, searchable by name, topic and a variety of ways.

CHILD MAINTENANCE

The Child Support Act 1991, Text and Commentary by Jonathan Montgomery, Sweet & Maxwell

The Child Support Handbook by Alison Garnham and Emma Knights, CPAG

The Child Support Act 1991 – A Practitioner's Guide by David Burrows, Butterworths

Money and Family Breakdown by Martha Street, LAG

'Child Maintenance - The Child Support Act 1991' by District Judge Roger Bird, 1993, *Family Law*

Child's Pay The Complete Guide to the Child Support Act 1991 and its Subordinate Legislation by Nicholas Mostyn, Family Law Bar Association

Child Maintenance: A Guide to the Child Support Act 1991 by Chris Bazell, Carolyn Pilmore-Bedford, and Ian Lomax, Tolley

SPECIALIST LAW UPDATES

Practitioners Guide to Child Law	edited by Remy Zentar Manchester Polytechnic
Family Law Reports	Justice of the Peace
Family Court Reports	Jordans, Family Law
Practitioner Child Law Bulletin	Longmans
Journal of Child Law	Tolley
Children Act News	DHSS
Family Law Directory	Jordans, Family Law
Seen & Heard	NAGALRO
Practice Notes Series	Cavendish Publishing Ltd

20 Improving Law, Skills and Practice

Child law changes rapidly. As this edition is being written, there is a new Adoption Bill before Parliament. It is necessary for lawyers to keep their law up to date, and to constantly improve skills. Child law involves keeping abreast of developments in medicine and psychology and in parenting skills, and maintaining a list of resources to which child clients and families may be referred.

It helps to belong to organisations which provide information and assistance, and in those areas of the country where child law practitioners may find themselves isolated, meeting others provides moral support within a network of colleagues.

20.1 Inter-disciplinary associations

Association of Lawyers for Children

    Secretary, Jeremy Barley, 163-165 How Street, Walthamstow, London E17 3AL. Tel 0181 520 8632.

British Association for Adoption and Fostering

    Secretary, Skyline House, 200 Union Street, London SE1 OLX.

    Tel 0171 407 8800; Fax 0171 403 6970.

British Association for the Study and Prevention of Child Abuse and Neglect (BASPCAN)

    National Office Administrator, 10 Priory Street, York, YO1 1EZ. Tel 01904 613605.

Guardians *Ad Litem* Steering Group (NAGALRO)

    c/o National Childrens' Bureau, 8 Wakeley Street, London EC1V 7QE.

    Tel 0171 278 9441.

IRCHIN
23a Hawthorne Drive, Heswall, Wirral, Merseyside L61 6UP.
Tel 0151 342 7852.
Local GAL and Solicitor Groups
Check with local Panel Managers.
Solicitors Family Law Association
Secretary, Mary L'Anson, PO Box 302, Keston, Kent.
Tel 0168 985 1227.

20.2 The Law Society's Children Panel

Practitioners specialising in representation of children and their families in public or private law matters need post-qualification experience in child and family work, a sound knowledge of child law, an understanding of child development, and skill in communicating with children.

Children Panel membership is a recognition of specialist training and experience, and also constitutes one of the criteria for claiming enhanced remuneration in specified circumstances under the Legal Aid Scheme. Many people, including the courts and guardians ad litem, instruct Children Panel solicitors in reliance on their expertise.

Solicitors wishing to be accepted for membership of the Children Panel need to have appropriate qualifications, acquire the necessary training, gain sufficient relevant experience and, finally, pass a selection interview. Children Panel Training courses cover a wide range of the topics necessary for the representation of children and their families. They are useful for all family lawyers, solicitors or legal executives; and, as an added bonus, they form the basis of qualification for Panel membership.

Information about the Children Panel, lists of training courses, and application forms can be obtained from Christine Caswell or Michael Barstow at The Law Society, Ipsley Court, Redditch, Worcestershire, B98 OTD.

20.3 Accreditation of family lawyers

Currently, the Law Society is considering the accreditation of family lawyers, and has issued a consultation document setting out draft proposals for criteria for registration.